John Edgar Wideman

John Edgar Wideman

Reclaiming the African Personality

Doreatha Drummond Mbalia

SUP

Selinsgrove: Susquehanna University Press
London and Toronto: Associated University Presses

Associated University Presses
440 Forsgate Drive
Cranbury, NJ 08512

Associated University Presses
25 Sicilian Avenue
London WC1A 2QH, England

Associated University Presses
P.O. Box 338, Port Credit
Mississauga, Ontario
Canada L5G 4L8

The paper used in this publication meets the requirements
of the American National Standard for Permanence of Paper
for Printed Library Materials Z39.48-1984.

Library of Congress Cataloging-in-Publication Data
Mbalia, Doreatha D.
  John Edgar Wideman : reclaiming the African personality / Doreatha
Drummond Mbalia.
      p.   cm.
  Includes bibliographical references and index.
  ISBN 0-945636-78-4 (alk. paper)
  1. Wideman, John Edgar—Criticism and interpretation.
2. Personality and culture—United States.   3. American fiction–
African influences.   4. Afro-Americans in literature.   5. Afro
-Americans—Psychology.   6. Psychology in literature.   7. Narration
(Rhetoric)   I. Title.
PS3573.I26Z77   1995
813'.54—dc20   94-47088
                                                      CIP

To all people of African descent,
with love and commitment

Contents

Preface

With the problems of exploitation and oppression confronting people of African descent becoming more and more acute with each passing day, those authors who attempt to address these dilemmas in their canon become role models for us all. John Edgar Wideman is one such author. Although his early works are disappointingly Eurocentric, his later works document his efforts to reclaim the African Personality. These later works, *the stories of john edgar wideman* in particular, reflect Wideman's awareness that no matter where African people live throughout the world, they share a common oppression and a common history. These later works also demonstrate that change does indeed occur, that African people, no matter how far outside the fold they may have wandered, can return and redeem themselves by servicing African people and their communities.

Writers such as Wideman do, however, risk the loss of popularity or the possibility of never gaining popularity because they use their works to explore the various crises plaguing the African community and to criticize the United States for causing these crises. Nevertheless, they take the risk. Like all great writers, they blend art and politics in order to bring sweetness and light to the world in general and to their people in particular, for they understand that it is the people—the everyday, hardworking masses—who are the makers of history. And, ultimately, the people will be the ones who give thanks and praise to those, like Wideman, who come to their aid.

Forward Ever, Backward Never. The struggle continues.

Acknowledgements

I would like to thank the following individuals and the university that made this work possible:

Chester Fontenot and the University of Illinois-Urbana for their guidance and financial support made possible by the University of Illinois Chancellor Minority Fellowship Award, 1990–91.

The Mbalia family, for excusing my many physical, sometimes mental, absences.

The struggle of African people, for giving me the ideological perspective needed to write such a study.

John Edgar Wideman

1

John Edgar Wideman: Reclaiming the African Personality

> "When you kill the ancestor you kill yourself."
> —Toni Morrison

John Edgar Wideman published his major works between 1967 and 1992. Thematically and structurally, these works reflect the author's evolution from one who is dominated by the history, culture, and language of Europe to one who accepts and appreciates African history, culture, and language. *A Glance Away* and *Hurry Home*, Wideman's first two novels, are the products of an African writer who is immersed in the western literary tradition. *Hurry Home*, for example, chronicles the life of an African male who has been so influenced by European culture that he begins to see with the eyes of a European, looking at the demeaning and hard work of a shoeshine boy as "romantic."[1] Structurally too it reflects an author whose audience is European and whose interest is in impressing that audience. Major parts of the novel are inscribed with "foreign" quotes (the inscription for the first part of the novel reads "muertries / De la langueur goutee a ce mal d'etre deux'"). These quotes are obstruse in their meaning and relevance to the African community. *Philadelphia Fire*, one of Wideman's last major works to date, is significantly different from the early ones, both thematically and structurally. It reflects the writing of an author who appreciates, respects, and embraces African life and culture and who has concern for African people. The title of the novel itself—reflecting the circumstances surrounding the bombing of a house occupied by members of an activist African organization—is sufficient proof. Structurally, Wideman sees the need to burn down the western literary standards that have ghettoized

15

his works up to this point. Using narrative techniques such as the triple-voiced narrator to reflect the collective voice represented in traditional African societies, Wideman imbues his text with meaning and structure relevant to the African community. Wideman's process of decentering himself from European life and culture and centering himself within African life and culture is the subject of this study.

There are several terms that describe this process. Two of the more modern concepts are "Eurocentricity" and "Afrocentricity". To be Afrocentric or African-centered means placing Africa, its culture, history, and values at the center of the African's existence. The term does not mean that one rejects European influences. Rather, the African, centered in his own culture, may extract the positive elements from cultures other than his own, including European culture. Doing so helps him to learn and develop. On the other hand, an African who is Eurocentric or European-centered is one who places Europe, its culture, history, and values at the center of his existence. He looks at the world as if he were a European. He lets Europe determine his identity and worth and the identity and worth of all people of African descent.

In 1980 Molefi Kete Asante, in a book entitled *Afrocentricity: The Theory of Social Change*, introduced the term Afrocentricity. According to him,

> The psychology of the black person without Afrocentricity has become a matter of great concern. Instead of looking out from his own center, the non-Afrocentric person operates in a manner that is negatively predictable. His images, symbols, lifestyles, and manners are contradictory to himself and thereby destructive to his personal and collective growth and development. Unable to call upon the power of his ancestors, because he does not know them; without an ideology of his heritage, because he does not respect his own prophets; he is like an ant trying to move a large piece of garbage only to find that it always falls back on him.[2]

This description of the African who is non-Afrocentric is one that aptly describes John Edgar Wideman in his early writings. These writings record the history of an author who has been taught to hate his culture, taught to hate himself and all those who look like him. Wideman now acknowledges his early self-

hatred and attributes his Eurocentric view to the education he
received at the University of Pennsylvania:

> At Penn I became a better player, but I paid a steep price for that. . . .
> Teachers, coaches, nearly everyone important in the white university
> environment, urged me to bury my past. I learned to stake too much
> of who I was on what I would become, lived for the day I could
> look back, look down on Reds and everybody else in Melton Park, in
> Homewood. (*Brothers* 226–27)[3]

There is, however, evidence within Wideman's own works that his
Eurocentric perspective began much earlier than his University
experience. Seemingly, his family's own rejection of "hard core"
African features and African ways tenderized and seasoned him
for the non-Afrocentric education he subsequently received at
Penn.

One of the best insights into the forging of Wideman's non-
Afrocentric view is *Brothers and Keepers,* a work in which Wideman
attempts to explain how his brother Robby's path to prison for
armed robbery was laid out for him by the race and class reality
of U.S. society. But more important for this study, *Brothers and
Keepers* is a book "about a writer who goes to prison to interview
his brother but comes away with his own story" (*Brothers* 78). At
one point in the book, Wideman explains the difference knowing
his history would have made in helping him to appreciate his
Africanness:

> I adopted the strategy of slaves, the oppressed, the powerlessness. I
> thought I was running but I was fashioning a cage. Working hand in
> hand with my enemies. Knowledge of my racial past, of the worldwide
> struggle of people of color against the domination of Europeans
> would have been invaluable. History could have been a tool, a support
> in the day-to-day confrontations I experienced in the alien university
> environment. History could have taught me I was not alone, my situ-
> ation was not unique. Believing I was alone made me dangerous, to
> myself and others. (32–33)

Not knowing his history made him divorce himself totally from
his identity, culture, and family. Perhaps it also played a decisive
role in his choice of female companionship, for Judy, his wife, is
a European, and his relationship with and marriage to her occurs

in this early, Eurocentric phase of his life. During this stage, with Wideman's limited knowledge of his heritage, he chose to be as much like the European as possible:

> Just two choices as far as I could tell: either/or. Rich or poor. White or black. Win or lose. I figured which side I wanted to be on when the Saints came marching in. Who the Saints, the rulers of the earth were, was clear. My mind was split by oppositions, by mutually exclusive categories. Manichaeism, as Frantz Fanon would say. To succeed in the man's world you must become like the man and the man sure didn't claim no bunch of nigger relatives in Pittsburgh. (27–28)

Wideman's ability in *Brothers and Keepers* to analyze himself is made possible by the re-education process that he undergoes. It is a detoxification process that enables him to shed his old European-centered frame of reference and reclaim his African personality. This he is able to do only after immersing himself in his culture, including discovering his family history and studying the literature of African people.

African historians and politicians have referred to this "detoxification" process by using various terms, including Afrocentricity and its opposite, Eurocentricity. Moreover, that W. E. B. Du Bois, Marcus and Amy Jacques Garvey, Frantz Fanon, Malcolm X, and Kwame Nkrumah and others have all described the essence of the concepts, though the terms they use may be unfamiliar, is significant in pointing out the crisis that the African has experienced since the African Holocaust.[4] That crisis can be described as a history of exploitation and oppression caused by capitalism.[5] Each of the African historic giants mentioned above have all ultimately pinpointed capitalism, including its system of education, as that which has caused some Africans to hate themselves. And each have implied or expressly admitted that until the conditions change—until the eradication of the exploitation and oppression of African people—terms such as Afrocentricity will continue to arise.

Since the essence of the concepts of Afrocentricity and Eurocentricity is not new—only the terms are new—it would be useful to highlight the conceptual forerunners of these terms. Doing so would offer convincing proof that since the slave trade some African people have been made so ashamed of their history and culture that they have attempted to disassociate themselves from them and to accept the history and culture of people of European descent as the only "legitimate" ones. That is, by tracing the evolution of the concepts, the reader gains a clearer insight into John Edgar Wideman.

In 1900, with the publication of *The Souls of Black Folks,* W. E. B. Du Bois introduced the world to the concept of double consciousness:

> The Negro is a sort of seventh son, born with a veil, and gifted with second-sight in this American world,—a world which yields him no true self-consciousness, but only lets him see himself through the revelation of the other world. It is a peculiar sensation, this double-consciousness, this sense of always looking at one's self through the eyes of others, of measuring one's soul by the tape of a world that looks on in amused contempt and pity. One ever feels his twoness,— an American, a Negro; two souls, two thoughts, two unreconciled strivings; two warring ideals in one dark body, whose dogged strength alone keeps it from being torn asunder.[6]

Du Bois's "double consciousness" theory accurately describes the crisis that Africans worldwide experience because of their powerlessness and, as a consequence, their lack of self-dignity, both of which cause them to be so mindful of how others see them that they allow those others to define them. With all the stereotypes that may accompany the other's perception, this schizophrenic existence is indeed, as Du Bois writes, "a peculiar sensation."

Marcus Garvey explained in 1917 that the Africans' powerlessness results from their lack of control of their homeland, for, according to him, it's the ownership and control of land from which a people derive power, and the dignity that naturally follows. The African "owns" land—Africa—but because of neocolonialism has no real (that is, economic) control of it. Garvey's solution was the reclamation of Africa for African people: Pan-Africanism. In 1917, he established the Universal Negro Improvement Association and African Community's League (U.N.I.A-A.C.L.) to unite the four hundred million Africans throughout the world to regain control of Africa during a time in which Africa was dominated by European colonization. The slogan of the U.N.I.A. was "Africa for the Africans, Those at Home and Those Abroad":

It falls to our lot to tear off the shackles that bind Mother Africa. Can you do it? You did it in the Revolutionary War. You did it in the Civil War; You did it at the Battles of the Marne and Verdun; You did it in Mesopotamia. You can do it marching up the battle heights of Africa. Let the world know that 400,000,000 Negroes are prepared to die or live as free men. Despise us as much as you care. Ignore us as much as you care. We are coming 400,000,000 strong. We are coming with our woes behind us, with the memory of suffering behind us—woes and suffering of three hundred years—they shall be our inspiration. My bulwark of strength in the conflict for freedom in Africa, will be the three hundred years of persecution and hardship left behind in this Western Hemisphere.[7]

Not to strive for Pan-Africanism, according to Garvey, would leave Africans vulnerable not only to the exploitation of their labor, but also the denigration and demoralization of their character, leaving them to imitate the European: in dress, in deed, in thought. In "An Appeal to the Conscience of the Black Race to See Itself," he states:

There is no progress in aping white people and telling us that they represent the best in the race, for in that respect any dressed monkey would represent the best of its species, irrespective of the creative matter of the monkey instinct. The best in a race is not reflected through or by the action of apes, but by its ability to create of and by itself. It is such a creation that the Universal Negro Improvement Association seeks.

Similarly, Amy Jacques Garvey, in an article appearing in *Negro World*, 10 July 1926, criticized those Africans who "choose the easier route" of aping Europeans instead of working to build up their own race:

Too much cannot be said in denouncing the class of "want-to-be-white" Negroes one finds everywhere. This race-destroying group are dissatisfied with their mothers and with their Creator. Mother is too dark "to pass" and God made a mistake when he made black people. With this fallacy uppermost in their minds, they bleach their skins and straigten their hair in mad efforts to look like their ideal type. . . . It is the way of the weakling. . . . This urge for whiteness is not just a mental gesture, it is a slavish complex, the remnant of slavery, to look like "Massa." To speak like him, even to cuss and drink like him.[8]

While Du Bois's as well as Marcus and Amy Garvey's statements help to clarify the "crisis of the African personality" that Africans experience because of their powerlessness, Frantz Fanon's classic work, *The Wretched of the Earth,* is invaluable in detailing the process of decolonization (i.e., detoxification) that the African undergoes once he becomes knowledgeable of his history and culture. Fanon was a psychiatrist, educated in France and imbued with capitalist values, who was assigned to a hospital in Algeria by the French during the French-Algerian war in the 1950s.[9] Though he went, in fact was chosen to go, because of his Eurocentric perspective, he soon became African-centered and supported the Algerian people's right to liberation from French colonialism. Fanon understood personally the process of moving from Eurocentricity to Afrocentricity. He uses the term "decolonization" to describe this process:

> Decolonization never takes place unnoticed, for it influences individuals and modifies them fundamentally. It transforms spectators crushed with their inessentiality into privileged actors, with the grandiose glare of history's floodlights upon them. It brings a natural rhythm into existence, introduced by new men, and with it a new language and a new humanity. Decolonization is the veritable creation of new men. But this creation owes nothing of its legitimacy to any supernatural power; the "thing" which has been colonized becomes man during the same process by which it frees itself.[10]

This decolonization process is necessary, according to Fanon, because the "native" has been taught to hate himself, his history, his culture. The African intellectual is a specific target of this education process, for it is he, as a part of the Du Boisian "Talented Tenth," who will lead the African masses:

> The colonialist bourgeoisie, in its narcissistic dialogue, expounded by the members of its universities, had in fact deeply implanted in the minds of the colonized intellectual that the essential qualities remain eternal in spite of all the blunders men may make: the essential qualities of the West, of course. The native intellectual accepted the cogency of these ideas, and deep down in his brain you could always find a vigilant sentinel ready to defend the Greco-Latin pedestal.[11]

Western education makes the African dream dreams of possession—possession of all that the oppressor has: "to sit at the settler's table, to sleep in the settler's bed, with his wife if possible." This dreaming is a reaction to being forced to stay in his place; "this is why the dreams of the native are always of muscular prowess; his dreams are of action and aggression. I dream I am jumping, swimming, running, climbing."[12]

Decolonization requires that the African intellectual immerse himself in his people and in his culture. Most often the process begins as a result of some personal crisis the intellectual experiences, a crisis that slaps him in the face, that reminds him of his inferior place in society despite his education. It is a personal experience that reveals to him that he (or his) is still a "nigger" no matter what his class status. This experience in turn jettisons him onto a path of rediscovery and reclamation, ultimately revealing to him

> that his life, his breath, his beating heart are the same as those of the settler. He finds out that the settler's skin is not of any more value than a native's skin; and it must be said that this discovery shakes the world in a very necessary manner. All the new, revolutionary assurance of the native stems from it. For if, in fact, my life is worth as much as the settler's, his glance no longer shrivels me up nor freezes me, and his voice no longer turns me into stone. I am no longer on tenterhooks in his presence; in fact, I don't give a damn for him.[13]

To clarify the relevance of the colonization process of Africans in Algeria to Wideman's early Eurocentric posture, Malcolm X's concept of "domestic colonialism" is quite useful. Malcolm X, orphaned while he was still in grade school, battled a life of crime until he was introduced to the Nation of Islam while in prison. From that moment on, he began studying his history and ultimately became a spokesperson for his people in the late 1950s and early 1960s. On 14 February 1965, Malcolm X spoke in Detroit at a meeting organized by the American Broadcasting Company. That speech, entitled, "After the Bombing," made it clear that Africans born in the U.S. were no less colonized than those born on the African continent: "Though the United States hadn't colonized the African continent, it had colonized 22 million blacks here on this continent. Because we're just as thoroughly colonized as anybody else."[14] Because Africans born in the U.S. are just as "thoroughly colonized" as Africans in Africa, Malcolm X used all of his speeches as forums to politically educate, to decolonize, to

Africanize the African in the U.S. One of the strategies Malcolm used to help educate Africans was to show them the connection between the plight of Africans on the continent and those in the diaspora:

> Now what effect does [the struggle over Africa] have on us? Why should the black man in America concern himself since he's been away from the African continent for three or four hundred years? Why should we concern ourselves? What impact does what happens to them have upon us? Number one, you have to realize that up until 1959 Africa was dominated by the colonial powers. Having complete control over Africa, the colonial powers of Europe projected the image of Africa negatively. They always project Africa in a negative light: jungle savages, cannibals, nothing civilized. Why then naturally it was so negative that it was negative to you and me, and you and I began to hate it. We didn't want anybody telling us anything about Africa, much less calling us Africans. In hating Africa and in hating the Africans, we ended up hating ourselves, without even realizing it. Because you can't hate the roots of a tree, and not hate the tree. You can't hate your origin and not end up hating yourself. You can't hate Africa and not hate yourself.
>
> You show me one of these people over here who has been thoroughly brainwashed and has a negative attitude toward Africa, and I'll show you one who has a negative attitude toward himself. You can't have a positive attitude toward yourself and a negative attitude toward Africa at the same time. To the same degree that your understanding of and attitude toward Africa become positive, you'll find that your understanding of and your attitude toward yourself will also become positive.[15]

Perhaps the African who did the most to understand and to attempt to solve the African's dilemma in regard to the psychological crisis he or she experiences as a result of capitalist education was Kwame Nkrumah. Nkrumah, first president of Ghana and foremost theoretician of Pan-Africanism in the twentieth century, introduced the term "African Personality" in 1960 and defined it as "the cluster of humanist principles which underlie the traditional African society.[16] It was his belief that Africans must reclaim this personality as their core and then "digest the Western and the Islamic and the Euro-Christian elements . . . and develop them in such a way that they fit into the African personality."[17] In other words, Nkrumah's advice was to place Africa at the center of the African's existence. He was not advocating a "going back to" some pre–slave trade existence, but a "moving forward to" a new reality by using the African's own history, culture, and values as the foundation of self.

According to Nkrumah, African people had become crisis-ridden due to their exploitation and oppression as a result of the rise of capitalism. They are taught to despise themselves, their history, their culture, and taught to view the world through the eyes of the European. Using himself as example, Nkrumah discusses the education he and other African students received as philosophy majors:

> I was introduced to Plato, Aristotle, Descartes, Kant, Hegel, Schopen-hauer, Nietzsche, Marx, and other immortals, to whom I should like to refer to as the university philosophers. But these titans were ex-pounded in such a way that a student from a colony could easily find his breast agitated by conflicting attitudes. . . .
>
> A colonial student does not by origin belong to the intellectual history in which the university philosophers are such impressive land-marks. The colonial student can be so seduced by these attempts to give a philosophical account of the universe that he surrenders his whole personality to them. When he does this, he loses sight of the fundamental social fact that he is a colonial subject. In this way, he omits to draw from his education and from the concern displayed by the great philosophers for human problems, anything which he might relate to the very real problem of colonial domination, which, as it happens, conditions the immediate life of every colonized African. . . .
>
> This defective approach to scholarship was suffered by different categories of colonial students. Many of them had been handpicked and, so to say, carried certificates of worthiness with them. These were considered fit to become enlightened servants of the colonial administration. The process by which this category of student became fit usually started at an early age, for not infrequently they had lost contact early in life with their traditional background. By reason of their lack of contact with their own roots, they became prone to accept some theory of universalism, provided it was expressed in vague, mel-lifluous terms.
>
> Armed with their universalism, they carried away from their univer-sity courses an attitude entirely at variance with the concrete reality of their people and their struggle.[18]

I've quoted Nkrumah at length because his statement appropri-ately describes the process of Europeanization that John Edgar

Wideman underwent. As indicated above, the fact that Nkrumah was a colonial student (Ghana was colonized by Great Britain and Nkrumah received a British, then a U.S. education) is of little relevance here since the African born in the U.S. lives under similar conditions, what Malcolm X and Nkrumah both called "domestic colonialism."

Wideman, like many other African people, first had to free himself from the Eurocentric mentality as a result of the domestic colonial education he received and then had to reclaim his African Personality. His reclamation process occurred in developmental stages, stages caused by a quantitative buildup of a number of factors, largely negative, involving family members, race concerns, and the writing process itself.

Of the dilemmas surrounding his family, the most impacting—even more than his grandmother's death, was that involving his youngest brother Robby. Robby's imprisonment for armed robbery and murder forced Wideman to come to terms with his own life, to ask the question: How can two members of the same nuclear family take such divergent paths in life? At the time he hears of Robby's "crime," Wideman is living in Laramie, Wyoming, thousands of miles from Pittsburgh: "We came out here [Wyoming] for what seemed like good reasons at the time, but it was another semiconscious break."[19] In *Brothers and Keepers,* he states:

> The distance I'd put between my brother's world and mine suddenly collapsed. The two thousand miles between Laramie, Wyoming, and Pittsburgh, Pennsylvania, my years of willed ignorance, of flight and hiding, had not changed a simple truth: I could never run fast enough or far enough. Robby was inside me. Wherever he was, running for his life, he carried part of me with him. (4)

While Wideman was running—from his Africanness, physically and psychologically, Robby was left "holding the bag," wallowing in all the problems of inner city life Wideman left behind. Not willing (or not having the opportunity) to sacrifice self and dignity and pride as an African man, Robby had only one choice: survival in the ghetto whether that meant getting over on the system or not. In one of the many conversations he had with Wideman while in prison, Robby acknowledges both the choices and the consequences of the choices that he and his brother made:

No way Ima be like the rest of them niggers scuffling and kissing ass to get by. Scuffling and licking ass till the day they die and the shame is they ain't even getting by. They crawling. They stepped on. Mize well be roaches or some goddamn waterbug. White man got em backed up in Homewood and he's sprinkling roach powder on em. . . . You know what I'm talking about. Don't tell me you don't, cause we both running. (*Brothers* 152)

At one point in *Brothers and Keepers,* Wideman writes that he at first thought he was writing the book to record Robby's story and, instead, came away with his own. And Robby's statement above acknowledges that both of them were running: Wideman away from self; Robby away from the police. Wideman seems to have committed the most serious crime, as he himself admits:

Were my visits to prison about freeing him or freeing myself from the doubt that perhaps, after all, in spite of all, maybe my brother has done more with his life than I've done with mine. Maybe he's the better man and maybe the only way I can face that truth about him, about myself, is to demystify the secret of his survival. Maybe I'm inside West Penn to warm myself by his fire, to steal it. Perhaps in my heart of hearts or, better, my ego of egos, I don't really want to tear down the walls, but tear my brother down, bring him back to my level, to the soft, uncertain ground where my feet are planted. (202)

It is as if Robby is the psychoanalyst and Wideman his patient, Robby the visitor and Wideman the prisoner, since it is the former who helps Wideman to confront his history, who helps to raise Wideman to another level of consciousness while Wideman attempts to "bring [Robby] back to my level." In another of the many self-revelatory sessions that Wideman has while visiting his brother, Robby teaches him about the nature of a "good nigger" vs. that of a man:

Yeah. I was a stone mad militant. . . . Mommy and them got all upset cause I was in the middle of the school strike. I remember sitting down and arguing with them many a time. All they could talk about was me messing up in school. You know. Get them good grades and keep your mouth shut and mind your own business. Trying to tell me white folks ain't all bad. Asking me where would niggers be if it wasn't for good white folks. . . . What it all came down to was be a good nigger and the white folks take care of you. (114)

One can imagine that the advice "Mommy and them" tries to give Robby was the same they gave Wideman, only Wideman listened and believed: "be a good nigger and the white folks take care of you."

Robby also helps his brother to understand that Wideman is not to blame for his running; that neither of them are. It is the society that shapes the person. Robby's graduation speech—he had completed the A.S. degree program in prison—makes just this point:

> The theme of our program today is "The world shapes and is to be shaped." I find this to be very appropriate. Because the world we were raised in has helped to shape many of the attitudes of us graduates here today. Most of us grew up in the ghettos of Pittsburgh and the surrounding area. (*Brothers* 240)

And if you are an African growing up without knowledge of your history that means, as Carter G. Woodson wrote over fifty years ago, that someone else can control your destiny, can teach you to hate your own history and culture, but to love the master's history and culture:

> When you determine what a man shall think you do not have to concern yourself about what he will do. If you make a man feel that he is inferior, you do not have to compel him to accept an inferior status, for he will seek it himself. If you make a man think that he is justly an outcast, you do not have to order him to the back door. He will go without being told; and if there is not a back door, his very nature will demand one.[20]

Wideman's teaching experience also played a significant role in sparking him to reclaim his African Personality. In fact, it was one of the first events to do so. (Though of much more significance, Robby's spark came later, after Wideman had left the University of Pennsylvania and was working at the University of Wyoming in Laramie.) Wideman refers to two teaching-related events in particular: his preparing to teach Afro-American literature while still at Penn and his editing a Norton Anthology of African-American literature. Both occur during the sixties, a time when African people—petty bourgeois and mass—were discovering or rediscovering their roots:

The sixties brought that whole necessity to examine one's own race and one's own background. I was part of that. By 1968 I was teaching at the University of Pennsylvania, and a group of black students asked me to start a course in Afro-American literature. I hemmed and hawed because I didn't know anything and I had my own writing to worry about and I didn't want to get involved in the work to put together a decent class and I didn't want to do it in a off-hand manner either. So there they sat in front of me and I suddenly heard myself giving them all the excuses, "That's not my field, and I don't know it, and I have my own work." I sounded like such a punk, I sounded like the very voice that had turned so many *people* back that I stopped short in the middle of all my excuses and said, "Yes, I'll do it, sure." It was the eye contact, *it was the sense of myself sitting out there listening to me,* that did it. That was a very important moment and I think my reading began to be quite serious at that point.[21]

The italicized word and clause are key to understanding Wideman's change of mind in regard to teaching an African-American literature course, for they reveal the nature of his audience. These students who come to him are obviously African. This fact aids him in connecting himself with them, in fact, in seeing himself as one of them, sitting in their seats. And seeing himself as them, he's able to feel what they feel, to desire what they desire—knowledge of themselves, their history, their culture, his culture. This step is an important early one for Wideman because it is through his commitment to the youth that he learns his own history, that he is sparked to evolve from a Eurocenteredness to an African-centeredness. Of course, this evolution also impacts upon the writing process; it frees him from the constraints of the Western literary tradition and centers him within the African tradition, a tradition which has its own standards that are always being creatively renamed and revised. In preparing for and teaching this class, but most important, in preparing for the transition from the aping of post-modernist European writers such as T. S. Eliot to the creative, self-assured African writer he becomes beginning with the Homewood Trilogy, Wideman began to appreciate his race, his culture, himself:

I did my homework for the [Norton] anthology and the course, and then I continued teaching the course. It became a special love. I continue to teach Afro-American literature. So, it has now been over four-

teen years—fifteen years—that I have been thinking about Black
writers and my interest has burgeoned to Caribbean and African
literature. . . . Afro-American writing was a serious academic concern,
on the one hand; on the other, it was a kind of great celebration, an
eye opener, an awakening, a feast.[22]

His "awakening" sparked Wideman to analyze his own personal
history, including his writings, to see where he and them fit within
African culture. Both came up short. After *The Lynchers* Wideman
does not publish his next novel, *Hiding Place,* until 1981, eight
years later. During this hiatus, he begins to study African history
and literature in order to discover his place within his own cultural
and literary heritage and to speak to his own people:

At a certain point in my writing career (if you want to call it that), I
made a decision. I had done three books, worked very hard, as hard
as I could, and they represented my ability to think through certain
problems; they represented my concerns as I wrote them. Also they
were for me a real laboratory. I was learning how to write. But after
those three books, I decided that I wanted to include other dimen-
sions in my writing. I wanted to do some things that I had not accom-
plished before. I wanted, number one, to reach out to levels of
audience that perhaps the earlier works had excluded.[23]

Of course, these "levels of audience" that Wideman refers to are
the African audiences. A significant change indeed. For it is the
choice of audience that determines the choice of subject-matter.
The two are dialectically connected.
One of the works Wideman reads during this transition period
that seems to have exerted a great deal of influence on his thinking and writing—his establishing an African voice—was Albert
Murray's *Stomping the Blues.* In his review of this work, Wideman
praised Murray for his ability to reject mainstream, i.e., Euro-
centered, writing and create his own unique African voice:

The expressive arts produced by Black Americans are informed by
rituals one of whose prime purposes is to transcend the limits and
boundaries imposed by the power of the majority society. Bursting
categories as basic as time and space, an alternate version of reality is
formed as Black people live their lives outside of the "mainstream"
of American culture. What Murray attests to is the power of these

alternative versions, how they shatter the complacencies of a main-stream, how the notion of a placid, separate, abiding mainstream is a fiction once you go below the surface—whether of language or music—and ask a few of the right questions.[24]

Murray's work may have been the catalyst for Wideman's transposition of James Baldwin's classic statement. What Wideman avows in his study of his work is the dialectical relationship between knowing one's history and knowing one's self, that knowing yourself is conditioned upon knowing your people, that "when you kill the ancestor, you kill yourself." (Or: "If you don't know your mama's name, you don't know your own name.") What Wideman learns is the importance of defining reality from one's own perspective. The African sees the world from his own center and tells the story of his life through his own eyes and in his own words.

Wideman's African-centeredness empowers him to re-evaluate his own life and works, allowing him to discern stages of evolution that he underwent: "I probably believe that more than most people that the notion of a stable, underpinning personality is itself a fiction. That people have different stages and go through different personas and they are really drastically different in the sense that you could talk about one person's life as many lives."[25] In Wideman's first life, his consciousness of himself as an African is so weak that he often depicts the European male—degenerate as he may be characterized—as the father of the African. It seems more his wish, his dream to be "white" with a Clark Gable type as his father, which blinds him to such an extent. And so what if it is a fantasy, for the early Wideman there is little or no difference between fantasy and reality. This message is conveyed in Hurry Home:

> In the novel this happens through an imaginary voyage, but I feel very strongly that people have this capacity to move over time and space in just such an empathetic way. It's almost silly to talk about whether it's a fantasy or whether it's happening because all of our experience has that same collapsible quality. It's a question of trying to blur that line between dream and reality.[26]

Since the only way Wideman can make himself a European is to make his father one through fantasy, Wideman must reduce reality to fantasy. This is what he does in his early literature. In Hurry

Home it makes no difference whether Cecil is experiencing reality or whether he's imagining all that happens. Reality and fantasy are one and the same.

There are other examples of Wideman's game playing with reality. His depiction, during this stage in particular, of African male characters who prefer European or very fair-skinned African women is a case in point. Lovemaking is the center of the relationship, at least in his novels. And this lovemaking between the African male and the European female sometimes occurs under a white sheet, blocking out the rest of the world, or under the female's hair, creating a tent under which both can hide from the predominantly negative attitudes toward interracial relationships that still exist in U.S. society.

In the early literature as well, the intellectual who is writer enjoys an elitist position. He is special and deserves the adoration of the reader. Rather than serve the people, the writer is removed from the people and thinks they should serve, or at least admire, him. This point of view is not surprising at all since, at this time, Wideman "thought writing was something that was connected with Europe. The matter of Europe. I didn't want to be a good American writer, let along a good black writer."[27] Of course, acceptance by those who have the power to publish, promote, and reward your writing has something to do with it. The critic James W. Coleman describes this dilemma that African writers have to wrestle with: "It is hardly unusual for writers or intellectuals to have difficulty in forging a relationship with the community when the culture in question lies outside the mainstream, because success and acceptance in the mainstream depend upon literacy defined in mainstream terms (in this case, proficiency in modernist and postmodernist forms and approaches)."[28] What Wideman, just as his predecessors, had to learn was how to find his own voice, no matter what price was paid in the process. In other words, he had first to understand that what was meant by "mainstream" was a Eurocentered frame defined by a ruling-class perspective, a frame which implied "a linguistic hierarchy, the dominance of one language variety over all others. This linguistic subordination extends naturally to the dominance of one version of reality over others."[29] Second, Wideman had to be strong enough to rebel against the mainstream because "if we don't fight the battle of defining reality in our own terms, then somebody else will always come along and do it for us."[30]

In his later works, Wideman is able to do just that: define reality from an African-centered perspective. Beginning with *Hiding Place*, Wideman uses a voice distinctly African in perspective. The African community is no longer conceived through the eyes of a European. African traditions are no longer described as primitive or ugly or dirty as they are in *A Glance Away*. Rather, they are what give us our strength to endure. Wideman describes his own reclamation process:

> In the later books also I began to understand how in using Afro-American folklore and language I didn't have to give up any of the goals that I was after when I was using more Europeanized and more traditional—literary traditional—devices and techniques. I didn't have to give up a thing. I could talk about the most complicated and sophisticated and intense moments and understandings and characters in the Afro-American idiom. That was a real breakthrough, but it was a breakthrough that didn't come accidentally. It was a result of study and concentration, and research in fact.[31]

Not only had Wideman nothing to lose ("I didn't have to give up a thing"), he had everything to gain: an understanding of the myths and stereotypes about African peoples and a reclaiming of his people's true history ("research in fact"). That is, he was born again, seeing without rose-tinted glasses or, in this case, Euro-centered glasses. With unobscured vision, he began to see himself connected to, not distinct from, other Africans. And once he realized that the African intellectual does have a role to play in the African community and will be accepted by it if he accepts it, one of the first questions he begins to ask himself is what is the role he as African intellectual can play in the community:

> There is a whole issue of what happens when anybody, any black person in this country, gains a skill, gains an education, gains some sort of power, whether it's a doctor, lawyer, businessman. How does that individual success relate to the fact that most people are far from successful in those economic terms, and how does success perpetuate the system that is in fact oppressing so many black people? And that issue is a vexed one and needs to be looked at and so *Brothers and Keepers* is an attempt to look at that as well. Systematically, what does

it mean that there can be one or two of us who are allowed to filter into professions, become college teachers, become writers? What is our responsibility, to ourselves, to the ones we left behind? Do we have to leave them behind? Are there ways that we can be successful without perpetuating the class and the racial hierarchy that produced this?[32]

Far from being unique or special in some superior way, the African intellectual is "allowed to filter into professions"; there are thousands of other qualified Africans who deserve that same opportunity, Wideman now understands. So what will those few who are lucky enough to get an education do for those who are not? That's the question Wideman asks and answers in *Reuben* and *Philadelphia Fire*. The writer who is Wideman can play a significant role in the community, first by writing the true history and culture of African people, by being "grounded in the culture" as Wideman himself states (*Brothers* 90–91), and by being an activist as well. One of the last, but significant, messages, that Wideman gives us in *Philadelphia Fire* is that writing alone is not enough: "Better to light one little candle than to sit on one's ass and write clever, irresponsible, fanciful accounts of what never happened, never will. Lend a hand. Set down your bucket. A siren screams. We should stop in our tracks. Walls are tumbling, burning-hot walls on tender babies" (157). Words alone are not enough; action is needed.

2

"Mean Mean Mean to be Free": The Evolution of Wideman's Consciousness

In Wideman's early novels, his consciousness of African culture and history and the plight of African people is based on a Euro-centered perspective. That is, he sees himself, his culture, his people through the eyes of a European. Such a distorted perspective, an anti-self perspective, makes him view writing as an act of superiority; forces him to see his audience as a European one; makes him choose "beat generation" themes (such as the Oedipus complex, the world as a wasteland, the intellectual's alienation from society); allows him to reject most things associated with African people; and forces him to write according to the literary standards of the West. By doing so, Wideman reveals his acceptance of the slave status and reflects the slave mentality of the African who experiences a personality crisis. Fanon describes this crisis in the following passage:

> The look that the native [the African slave] turns on the settler's [the slave master's] town is a look of lust, a look of envy; it expresses his dreams of possession—all manner of possession; to sit at the settler's table, to sleep in the settler's bed, with his wife if possible.[1]

Wideman's later works, however, reveal his rejection of the slave mentality and reflect the revolutionary mentality of an African who sees himself, his culture, his people through his own eyes—the eyes of an African. The title of this chapter, then, becomes meaningful in two contrasting ways. Unlike the runaway slave in Robert Hayden's poem "Runagate Runagate," the early Wideman runs away from his home (a place, a state of mind, an identity, a culture, a history) toward slavery (a foreign place, state of mind, identity, and culture). But the later Wideman—the Wideman who writes *Hiding Place,* a few stories in *Damballah,* some sections of *Sent for You Yesterday,* half of *Reuben,* and most of *Philadelphia Fire*— is the runagate who runs away from slavery toward freedom because he is no longer shell-shocked, abused, confused. He is the Runagate who avows: "And before I'll be a slave / I'll be buried in my grave."

That his early works imitate those of European post-modernist writers such as T. S. Eliot is a significant indication of Wideman's Euro-centeredness. According to O'Brien, "his academic training shows up in allusions to and imitations of the literary figures he admires, especially T. S. Eliot. *A Glance Away* echoes the early poetry of Eliot both in mood and style and has a central character who—Wideman admits—resembles Prufrock" (213).[2] It is not just a case in which "his academic training shows up"; all Africans who have gone to college have been trained from a Euro-centered perspective. But some have sifted through the training, retaining what is positive and rejecting what is negative. So, it is not just a case of academic training; it is also a matter of perspective. In an interview with Kay Bonetti, Wideman himself admits that he had his "priorities a little bit mixed up":

> I felt that I had to prove something about black speech for instance, and about black culture, and that they needed to be embedded within the larger literary frame. In other words, a quote from T. S. Eliot would authenticate a quote from my grandmother.[3]

To be authenticated by a European in any way was necessary for one like the early Wideman who believed that to be as much like the European was right. To be master of the "word"; to be the person who "says" that one thing is better than another, that one writer is better than another, that one race is better than another is to be more closely linked to the European than the African who is told, who does no telling. To choose a subject that was more germane to the European's reality than his own also would show them (the Europeans) that he was worthy of being accepted. To use the same narrative structure as that which is deemed correct—linear, not cyclic; European English, not African English; the author removed from, not involved in the story being told— is to be more like the European.

Perhaps the most telling sign of Wideman's early self-imposed isolation from his Africanness is his depiction of troubled European males as father figures to young African males. In *A Glance Away*, Robert Thurley, a Southern, European, alcoholic, homosexual intellectual, is both a main character and a father figure for the struggling African protagonist, Eddie. This is true despite the fact that Thurley sexually molests little African boys, "nigger, pickaninnies," as he calls them.

Just having Thurley in the novel speaking in his own voice reflects Wideman's Eurocentric point of view, because of what relevance are the intellectual musings, exemplified by the following passage, of a degenerate European to African people?

> [Thurley] swerved to avoid something dead on the roadside. Was it conscience, simply the old religious fear . . . ? The agenbite of inwit. He smiled, letting the quotation drain off the building intensity. Quotation is as close to reality as they can get. Was it Stendhal, or was it some aside in Rostov's glittering salon? Perhaps even Flaubert. Sounds like a conclusion he would come to after leafing through his trunk of *idees recus*.[4]

And of what significance to the African is the relationship between Thurley, his wife, and his best friend who at one time engaged in a ménage-à-trois?

Evidently, Wideman's concern is to show the underlying, fundamental similarity between human beings. That, yes, African and Europeans can meet on some abstract, harmonious ground, for on one occasion Wideman takes the time to philosophize about the humanity of Thurley and the possibility of some kind of unity forged between him and Eddie:

> But how could Eddie know that beneath his olive suit, within the flushed, white flesh was a consciousness just as acute, just as accusing, just as aware of the beast as Eddie's hate had made him. And if they could meet so powerfully, if the same anger could be shared, could not remorse and the act of forgiveness bind them just as tightly? (156)

It is Wideman's interest in integrating the European and the African which drives him so far as to depict Thurley as father figure to Eddie, a depiction that lacks the requisite motivation needed to make it even remotely plausible: "He had only the vaguest idea of Eddie's character, only Brother's garbled anecdotes and the

words passed in two short confrontations. But he also knew nothing would ever be able to separate him from the young man's
pain. He must help Eddie" (167). By the end of the novel, Thurley
takes control of Eddie, seeming to know Eddie better than
Brother, his best friend since childhood! Wideman has Brother
state, "I'll just follow Eddie if Bobbie [Thurley] thinks it's best and
probably he's right" (172). And perhaps what is most remarkable
is that Eddie allows himself to be led by the European, despite
his knowledge of Thurley's sexual exploitation of Brother. By the
end of the novel, structurally, Wideman mixes up the thoughts of
Eddie, Thurley, and Brother to create the integration that he
wishes to forge between the men in particular and the races in
general. The image of the fire as agent for melting the men into
one pot of Americanism is the last picture that Wideman leaves
with the reader. It is the fire that molds all three into one, as
Brother acknowledges: "They don't move. They cannot speak.
The flame crackles. I don't move, don't speak. All time, near then
far, near then far, near then far. The crickets stop. We are part
of the fire" (186).

Not only is Wideman's early rejection of Africanness illustrated
in this attempt to create a Jean Toomer-like world of no races,
just one human race, but also in his consistent ridicule of dark-
skinned, poor African people, in the same manner as racist Europeans. Africans are fat, black, sweaty, nappy-headed people who
love to dance:

> He [Tiny] was round, huge and round with rolls of black fat. Always
> sweating, . . . Talk about some colored people. Women with nets
> wrapped around the little, nappy hair they had, and the men sitting
> stiff in starched collars, like babies in high chairs with hard bibs under
> their chins. But that was only until the music started. . . . You think
> those Strip niggers can make a racket! Just go hear the sanctified one
> day. (127)

Wideman does not yet understand that by ridiculing African people, the African masses, he is ridiculing himself. Clearly the message conveyed in this first novel is that Wideman sees himself more
closely aligned with Europeans than his own people. There is even
the indication that Wideman wishes to be a European. In one
revealing scene in *A Glance*, Wideman relates the story of Eddie's
childhood when he was friends with a European named Joel.

After getting in a fight with the Europeans whom he hangs around with and who all gang up on him, Eddie walks home just as snow begins to fall: "He had smiled feeling the soft snow blot against his skin. All away, all washed away, closer, nearer" (101). The snow is not just soft and comforting, it is potentially transforming. In blotting his skin, the snow can remove the blackness and bring Wideman "closer, nearer" to the European.

In regard to Wideman's Euro-centeredness, *Hurry Home* evidences some of the same weaknesses in the author's overall consciousness of himself as an African as does *A Glance Away*. The audience of *Hurry Home* is still predominantly European. The novel is dedicated to Judy, Wideman's European wife; Part I is inscribed with a French quote that surely the average African would not be able to translate; and Part III is inscribed with a quote from Hermann Hesse's *Demian*, "so we bear everything in our soul that once was alive in the soul of men. Every god and devil that ever existed," as if by using the words of a European author Wideman can assure his audience of the validity of the African's need to accept himself and his past.

Once again the European is in a prominent, paternalistic position in the novel. Although not main characters, Wideman uses two Europeans as important characters in the story, characters who help the main character, Cecil Otis Braithwaite, better understand himself. Thanks to Webb, a homosexual European who has a son by an African woman, Cecil has the opportunity to discover himself, his roots. He learns of the Moors while in Spain and embarks on a trip to Africa. Unfortunately, Cecil does not see Webb as conduit, but as someone of greater importance than himself. A mentor or a father, perhaps: "I think at times I am on the edge of a great awakening or at least a realization. Something to do with understanding Webb. What do we share. Where have we been" (45).[5]

The absence of an African-centered perspective cannot only be gauged by a homosexual European male's role in aiding Cecil in understanding his Africanness, but also by the space and time Wideman devotes to presenting Webb's story. Not only is this story of a self-centered European who envies his African mistress' ability to write—a jealousy that eventually destroys their relationship—completely irrelevant to Cecil's growth and development and to the reader's understanding of that process, but also such a story is seemingly unfamiliar ground for Wideman, just as the Thurley-Al story in A Glance Away. Unless it is Wideman, an African man, who is jealous of his wife's (mistress') ability to write. Perhaps this conjecture makes more sense in relation to the space and time devoted to Webb's story.

A European mercenary, Albert's presence in the novel is, at first, just as perplexing. However, the significant point Wideman makes about him is that Albert wants to live in the past, to reclaim his past while Cecil wishes to escape his past, to live in the present. Of himself, Albert announces: "I'm an anachronism, friend. There's a certain security in this. Last of the race. A dinosaur" (54). Albert does not hesitate to pull out photos, reminders of a proud past: "Albert loving. Releasing from behind the stolid dikes a sheaf of photos he kept with him always, stuffed inside his offensively bold, open-throated plaid shirt" (63). Neither Wideman nor Cecil thinks proudly of his past, but instead is ashamed of it.

Just as in A Glance Away, another telling sign of Wideman's Eurocenteredness is his rejection of his Africanness despite the fact that it is this which brings the only true comfort and consolation he feels throughout the novel. In blaming his skin-color for his problems instead of his oppressors, Cecil prays for the relief that either whiteness or death brings: "O father, father forgive me, forget me, let me forget that I have skinned, that I have sinned, forget me Father, no more please for I am dying" (68). Since death is an option for him, but whiteness isn't, much of Cecil's thoughts are centered on death and dying, a concentration which makes him miss out on life. So instead of going about the business of either creating another son, or adopting one, Cecil goes through the novel whining about and mourning over his miscarried son, Simon, a son he at first did not even want. In fact, this worrying about things which he has no control over, instead of for those he does have control over—his life, his relationship with his wife, Esther, the African community—is a mourning which has its seeds in his frustrated attempts to be a European, a barrister just like the Europeans in his class, a useless writer like Webb who writes only for himself ("My book is all the things I spend so much energy preparing to say to someone but never do to anyone" [154]). Wideman does not yet understand that just as life is useless unless shared, so is writing, that one discovers self within the collective, not outside of it.

Once Cecil realizes he'll never be a European, he settles on being an "only" African, the kind that says, "I'm the only African in my neighborhood" or "I'm the only African in my class." "Choice two, choice two is unavoidable. Everyone likes to be thought of as unique, don't they. One of a kind, treated accordingly" (154). Such an unrealistic concentration on and promotion of self makes Cecil regress to a complete state of silliness; life becomes a game, and communication, rhyme: "Not bad for an im-prompt-too. I could rhyme forever, never ever lever sever fever. Eye rime" (154). Cecil becomes schizophrenic, living in his mind only.

It is only when Cecil gets involved with the community that he begins to heal himself, sew himself together. Interestingly, this wholing process begins with his job as a hairdresser in Constance's Beauty Shop for African men and women. The beauty parlor is as central to the African community as the barbershop, so it is quite significant that Wideman chooses the former because a part of Cecil's healing is in knowing what went wrong, how he was processed in the first place. At Constance's, Cecil creates the kind of hair-head-mind-consciousness that reflects brainwashing. By processing the African's hair, Cecil helps the oppressor to oppress the African. What Cecil and Wideman must figure out is the best kind of action to help African people; action that is progressive, not processing. For Wideman, he must move from a belief in art for arts sake, the emulation of European art, to purposeful art. Art can hurt (process) or help (progress) African people. It's not neutral. There's no middle ground. For Cecil, he must begin to accept himself (his identity, his roots, his people) for whom he is.

It is while at Constance's Beauty Parlor that his acceptance process begins. While there, Cecil is inundated with the music, the folksy talk, the smells and sights of the African masses: "All factions, contradictions, extremes not extinguished but harmonized, not blurred but made compatible by a force whose nature Cecil could not plumb. Was it blackness, some secret experience of the race, blood knowledge ineradicable" (164). It is while at Constance's that Cecil begins to make the connection between himself and other Africans: "Must I see myself in them to know myself to believe myself" (165). It is a connection that is certainly tenuous, but a connection nevertheless. One has only to juxtapose this probing and questioning, with Cecil's earlier clear rejection of himself as an African during his encounter with a shoeshine boy. In that instance, Cecil offends the shoeshine boy and thus the whole community because he sees himself as Other. His view of them, in fact, is the same as that held by the European; the shoeshine boy's work is entertaining, exotic even, labor that should be accompanied by music: "I would my fingers held some musical instrument—a guitar, a fiddle. I would play beside the boy, accompany him along the street. And each time we stopped to emblazon some customer a crowd would gather, watch him pop and flick and rub" (32).

However, it is through his conversation with his namesake, his Uncle Otis, that Cecil's acceptance of himself as a part of, not apart from, the African community is solidified. Through parables, Uncle Otis teaches Cecil that you can never "rise above" your people; such an act is synonymous with not living at all: "When I was younger, I used to love to climb utility poles. . . . But it was good just sitting secretly up there where nobody can touch you. Sometimes. I even thought no one could see me like I had really disappeared from the earth" (175). Like his destruction of a dog whose heart he took, Uncle Otis teaches Cecil the role the latter played in the destruction of his wife, Esther; Cecil took her heart. (That the dog is a part of this analogy shows how much Wideman has yet to grow on the question of women.) Both Otis and Cecil, in destroying others, destroyed themselves. This is one important lesson that Uncle Otis teaches Cecil. Another is the importance of action; the need to fight those who oppress you: "And slay them whenever you catch them. . . . And fight them until there is no more tumult or oppression. Koran 2:191; 193" (176).

Thus it is only by the end of the novel that the title takes on its full significance. The title, "Hurry Home," suggests the need to return quickly to one's roots, the source of one's identity in keeping with don l. lee's poem "Confessions of an Ex-Executive": "Back Again, Black Again, Home." Cecil must return to the brown arms that gave birth to him, that nourished him, the Branbury Arms, even if it means living at the bottom, the basement, as a janitor: "Cecil moved early in [the] darkness, that with a cat's feet he could go anywhere he wanted without bumping things or tripping. . . . The cool, dark air seemed to restore him, to right a balance" (10–11). And even Cecil's statement, the "direction was clear, but destination, even point of departure impossible to grasp," is key in our knowing that Cecil (Wideman) understands what he must do even though the final solution, the objective is unclear. After this novel, Wideman's focus will be more African-centered. His purpose will be not in trying to escape his Africanness, but in trying to discover it. So even though the novel ends with the words, "So Cecil dreamed," as if the whole experience (i.e., the plot of the novel) was nothing but a hallucination, we as readers know it was a learning experience for Wideman. Even dreams can teach. Like Cecil, Wideman learns an important lesson: he cannot isolate himself from the African community. Rather, he must accept his identity and struggle for a healthy, wholesome place in society.

If Wideman begins to question and to accept his identity in *Hurry Home,* in *The Lynchers* he researches the African's history and gets angry about the facts he discovers. Unlike the first two novels, *The Lynchers,* from the very beginning, lets the reader know that the subject matter is strictly concerned with African people, although the audience is still European. The "Matter Prefatory" sets the tone of the novel. It is a list of historical facts relating the African's treatment in the U.S. According to Wideman, "All the quotations are actually taken from newspapers and documents. I wanted to immerse the reader in a reality that for one reason or another he wasn't ready to accept, one which under normal circumstances would seem fantastic to him."[6] That the facts presented would seem fantastic to the reader, but, even more significant, that "he" wasn't ready to accept this reality lets us know that Wideman's audience is European. Yet, the "Matter Prefatory" does convince the reader that Wideman's primary concern is African people, and it even hints at the role that Wideman will come to embrace and to advocate for African intellectuals: one of activism. Coleman agrees:

> The "Matter Prefatory" is a crucial structural feature of *Lynchers* because it very forcefully supports a world-view that sets a high priority on attention to the black community and on activism as a remedy for the problems in that community. It clearly implies that black individuals need to play some kind of activist role in their community, even if they merely identify with it and interact with its members.[7]

For the first time, Europeans are not treated as Great White Fathers. In fact, the only European present in the novel is a policeman whom the four main characters plan to lynch, a minor expendable character. Clearly, the tone of the novel is one of anger, as Wideman himself admits:

I felt threatened. I felt very threatened, and the threat to me was not only personal, it was a threat to a whole people. I saw as lots of us did, paranoid versions of—well, not so paranoid—versions of a country that was just going to self-destruct because of its racism, and a country which was at kind of a crossroads and had to make some really basic choices. Was it going to move a little bit to accommodate new voices—young peoples' voices, black peoples' voices, voices of change—or was it going to puff up its chest and send out the immigrants to whip on the black people again. And I felt that threat very personally and tried to talk about it in *The Lynchers*.[8]

Evidently, Wideman has begun to research his history in detail and is angry, a natural first reaction for any African. Littleman, the ideologue and master planner of the novel, speaks of the anger Wideman feels: "How could you allow yourself to see the decay and dying without either killing white people or going mad? Above the rotting, steel boned seats he could see Afros floating, the soft teased hair of his people."[9]

Anger, however, prevents Littleman and the other African characters from seeing clearly. They are united in anger, not in ideology, despite the fact that each has character traits which are valuable to the group: Saunders, a fascination with family history and an objectivity that Wilkerson lacks; Wilkerson, education and subjectivity; Rice, subterfuge and disemblance; and Littleman, knowledge of his history and the commitment to act. Such a unity—one built on anger—leaves the group vulnerable to the weaknesses of one another as well as to the society. After discussions on how to "save" African people, they attack one another like enemies, making their plan unworkable from the start:

Littleman absolutely committed to the plan, teasing and slashing at the others with the authority his readiness gave to him. Saunders resentful because Littleman had something he needed badly and would relinquish it only on his own terms, terms Saunders must submit to. Wilkerson still fumbling, unable to see the plan except as a

joke or enormous threat. So Littleman piped and they paid. And the
chill air made them brittle as glass as they bumped awkwardly in the
music he played. Wilkerson wanted words to make them all laugh,
forget a moment the violence that drew them together. (49)

That the plan is doomed from the start, despite the good intentions of the four men (their recognition of the need for oneness
among African people and their attempt to bring it about), is
borne out by several other factors.[10] First, there is the misconcep-
tion that a unit, a group or an organization needs a person to lead,
the others to follow. Such a theory leaves the group vulnerable, for
once the leader is destroyed so is the unit. This is in fact the case
with the lynchers-to-be. When Littleman acts prematurely, then is
beaten up by policemen and carried off to jail, the group falls
apart. No one else is capable of leading. Wilkerson certainly is
not. Not only is his involvement motivated by selfish desires, but
also he doubts the plan: "I believe in his plan. It may free men
for an instant, create a limbo between prisons. But can the instant
be extended? Can it support life and society? I don't think Littleman cares. I don't think my father cared when he felt the need
to escape. He could run and that was enough" (72–73). This connection that Wilkerson makes with Littleman and his father is
neither incidental, nor accidental. In one regard, Littleman resembles Wideman's own brother Robby who felt that action was
needed. "My father" is Wideman himself who instead of staying
and struggling alongside Robby runs away, escapes. The "what I
am running from " is important. In another regard, running away
is something that Wideman's father does periodically. The "act of
running" is important: "Why am I here? . . . the need to embrace
my father, though for years I had accepted and tried to accustom
myself to the fact that I no longer had a father" (145).

Wilkerson's doubts about the plan is mirrored by his doubts
about his identity. Like Wideman himself during the writing of
this book, Wilkerson understands and acknowledges the theoretical, spiritual connection between himself and his African identity,
but is not yet comfortable with it. While Wilkerson teaches his
class African history, for instance, mouthing the names Mansa
Mansa and Lumumba, "the ghost of a white giggle is restless" in
his throat (84). The phrase "white giggle" is revealing: the idea
that laughing at the African is something whites [i.e., Europeans]

do. The idea that Wideman would laugh at himself! And like any foreigner to a culture, Wilkerson first sees African culture as exotic and attempts to identify with it by purchasing a dashiki and stooping to talk with an African born on the continent about lions. When the African haughtily responds, "No my good man, I have never seen a lion, outside a zoo that is" (83), Wilkerson is "off the smart alecky big lipped bastards for months after this foray, this sincere attempt to come to terms with my past." Not knowing much about his past reflects his lack of knowledge about himself: His journal entries reveal "almost nothing about its author"; and when he sees a reflection of himself, it is either scarred or the image makes him dizzy.

Neither Saunders nor Rice is capable of leading either. Rice tells the others lies (53) and Saunders is impatient, too quick to act/react, and burdened with intraracial color prejudice: "The whiteness in Wilkerson's complexion and features that yellow niggers like him wore so proudly in their mongrel faces, would always earn them crumbs from the Master's table" (156). It is a prejudice that prevents him from trusting Wilkerson to even execute his part of the plan: "Saunders asked himself how little of the enemy remaining was enough to taint. When the deal went down, when it was kill and be killed would Wilkerson make a clean break, shed his white man's ways, white man's blood" (156).

From the start then, it is clear that only Littleman can lead. Like Headeye in Henry Dumas's "The Ark of Bones," Littleman's physical characteristics are employed as metaphor for intelligence and leadership qualities: "Height of a twelve year old, heavy head and shoulders done in a heroic manner then stick legs added by a clumsy apprentice" (50–51). Physically, he appears abnormal because of his head size, but also because he is handicapped. Creating a big-headed cripple, Wideman wants the reader to understand the relationship between one's physical deprivation and one's level of consciousness. Second, Wideman wants his reader (remember the audience is European) to understand that when the society cripples Africans, it causes its own destruction.[11]

Littleman's rootlessness also equips him with leadership abilities. Having only "uneven mumblings of song" as "the family, the home, the child's glow of peace and innocence he had ever known" (124), he feels the blows of capitalist U.S.A. much more than the others, and this clarifies his vision as to the nature of the society and its impact on African people.

A third factor which ensures the failure of the plan from the beginning is the group's need to ensure against individual copout. It is an insurance needed because of the absence of ideological unity within the group. Since they ban together for different reasons, they "must build safeguards into the plan, minimize the possibility of individual cop out by maximizing the certainty that the one who fails cannot hurt the others and will himself be absolutely dealt with" (59).

The Lynchers then is a transition novel within Wideman's canon. It is betwixt and between two worlds: the Eurocentric and the Afrocentric. Wideman seeks the theoretical need for oneness among African people, but it is a oneness that is built on misconceptions. Littleman, for example, thinks that African people can empower themselves by repeating the acts of racist, ignorant Europeans: "When I talk about lynching, I'm talking about power" (61). Of course, lynching a European is not the solution, for the average, working European too has been molded by the same system. Then too Littleman (Wideman) seems unaware of his history, believing that African people have never united for a cause ("When have we ever risen up as a people, unified, resolved ready to die together. Never, never once in our pitiful history" [116]) and thinking that to lynch is to build an African nation (117).

Despite this weakness in the novel—Wideman's unsuccessful attempt to create a viable solution for the African's exploitation and oppression, the author does succeed in conveying his sincere interest in and commitment to discovering more about his roots: family, community, and race. And he does succeed in this novel in revealing his concern for African people in general. Unlike Cecil in *Hurry Home*, Littleman is fully aware of his identity, an awareness that equips him to see other Africans in the community as pitiful victims of exploitation and oppression, not as aggressive, violent men or exotic shoeshine boys who threaten his existence:

> Littleman nodded at the men around the ramshackle shoeshine stand. Six or seven sitting and standing, exiles from another planet huddling close to the wreckage of the elaborate machine which had dropped with them from the heavens. They projected confusion, their eyes and hands moved at the wrong speed, evidence of a subtle deterioration

of hidden, vital organs. Sucking on bottles of sweet soda pop, chewing candy bars. (119)

And by the end of the novel, Littleman (Wideman) seems to have come to the understanding that African people must be politically educated, not reacting to stimuli like zombies who do as they are told. For, in that case, they would be just as helpless and useless as they are presently. With Anthony, the hospital attendant, Littleman goes through the process of passing on, sharing, his knowledge of what it means to be an African in the U.S. It is a political education process that seemingly pays off in the end. Littleman succeeds in awakening Anthony's consciousness of himself as an African. When Anthony discovers that Littleman has been confined to the "looney" floor as a "political prisoner," he gets angry and begins smashing any and everything in his way: "His bony black wrist is a scythe as it slashes through bottles, vials, tubes, cups and glasses, all that sustains life in neat array atop the nurses' station" (264). This "rioting" is Anthony's gut reaction to his realization of himself as an exploited and oppressed human being. As the last line in the novel, the one concerning Anthony's act is a powerful revelation of Wideman's growing consciousness of himself as an African.

The anger—for Anthony, for Littleman, and for Wideman—is a necessary first step. The next step is to move beyond anger to considered, decisive action, the first stage of which is political education, first learning one's history and then sharing one's knowledge of African history and current events with others. Wideman will take his own advice, using the next three novels to learn about and to share his own family history.

The title of Wideman's fourth novel, *Hiding Place*, comes from an African-American spiritual: "Went to the Rock to hide my face / Rock cried out, No hiding place." The emphasis is on face; that is, one's Africanness. Following his own advice in *The Lynchers*, Wideman's message in this novel is that an African must confront and accept his history, his identity; not run from them like Cecil in *Hurry Home*.

There is an eight-year hiatus between the writing of *The Lynchers* and *Hiding Place*. During this time, Wideman studied the works of other African writers and wrote critical essays about what he learned. Coleman writes: "Several critical essays about black writ-

ing, most of them published during the eight-year hiatus between
Lynchers and *Hiding Place,* indicate what Wideman learned from
other black writers about black cultural resources and about
speaking in a black voice."[12] It makes sense too that Wideman
listened more closely to speech patterns of Africans. *Hurry Home*
gives us a clue. While Cecil is working in Constance's Beauty Parlor, he is surrounded by the African vernacular; the music, the
folksy talk of the patrons. Once Wideman begins to learn his
history, he accepts himself for whom he is. This then is an eye
opener and an "ear opener": he begins to see legitimacy and
beauty in what he is, what he does, what he says, and what he
hears. So it is this literature by other Africans that Wideman stud-
ies and, perhaps most important, his own eye-and ear-opening
experiences teach him that not only can he not hide from his
identity, but also he must face up to all the problems associated
with this acceptance. It teaches him too the value of his culture:
that it nurtures him, gives him strength, keeps him alive.

Hiding Place then is the first novel in which Wideman clearly
accepts his African identity. It is the first work in a trilogy (the
Homewood Trilogy) in which Wideman examines his own family
history, an examination that is straightforward, unclouded by a
contortionist structure or by heavy symbolism. Wideman's clear,
unencumbered writing suggests that the knowledge he learned
so impacted upon him that he wanted to record it clearly as a
historian would relate the facts of an event.[13] In an interview with
Bonetti, Wideman discusses just how much his family history af-
fected him:

> I reacted in a personal way to the examples of my mother, and my
> aunts and uncles, and my grandfather and the people who, as I wrote
> about and thought about and learned about them, came to be the
> most important people in my life again. I had kind of lost touch with
> them and lost touch with their importance. I was looking in other
> places for the nurturing and the wisdom and models. But coming
> back to them I found that they had taken the most dramatic kinds of
> chances. They had united their fate with mine. And as I looked
> around more carefully I found that that had occurred in no other
> arena of my life.[14]

By beginning with Clement's point of view, a view that is child-
like in its simplicity, Wideman gives us a mirror into the commu-

nity. Straight talk. Not the screened-out, judgmental view of the
intellectual or the adult. The setting too is important in this regard. What better place to hear the latest news— uncensored,
fully detailed—of the community than a barbershop. Then filter
it through the eyes of a young man with the mentality of an eight
year old and you have the rock bottom truth.[15]

Wideman's drive to know the truth, not run from it, empowers
him to create a plot in which the main character has to go back
to the source of his family history, at least the source since the
family was freed from slavery, in order to learn the importance
of confronting dilemmas associated with one's identity. Tommy,
after involving himself in armed robbery and murder, runs to
Bruston Hill, the roots of his people in Homewood: "This the top
of Bruston Hill. This the place in the stories all my people come
from" (39).[16] Like Wideman's own early act of writing about himself and his roots, Tommy's return is an unconscious recognition
of the need to know his history: "If he had reasons for picking
this jive place he surely didn't know what they might be. Didn't
know why or when his feet decided to climb Bruston Hill" (39).
This unconscious quest must turn into a conscious one—for
Tommy as well as Wideman. Once it does both will accept their
history and, in accepting, commit themselves to discovering more
about their kind: their family and their race. A commitment that
ultimately leads to problem-solving.

But the first steps in the process toward helping one's people
are what Wideman examines in *Hiding Place:* confrontation, acceptance, and commitment (at least in its embryo stage). It is a
process that always involves more than one individual. It takes at
least two to tangle, and for Tommy to grapple with his past, his
great aunt Bess must be his partner. And what an appropriate
partner she is. Bess is also running way from her past, but unlike
Tommy, hers is a mental, not physical, escape. Both Tommy and
Bess must learn the value of roots in sustaining them. Bess must
stop thinking that "all that old time stuff don't make me no never
mind" (82) and Tommy must stop thinking that the solution to
any problem is to run away: "All I need's a little time. Little peace
so I can stop running" (93). Bess's response to this type of talk is
to mock Tommy into realizing its absurdity: "Listen to you. Listen
at this poor child. The day you die is the day you stop running"

(93). This is the lesson Bess teaches Tommy; Tommy teaches Bess the same:

> Why you stay up here, old woman? You scared ain't you? You been just as scared up here as I been down there. And if I'm hiding, you're hiding too. But I'm hiding so I can run. You just hiding. You let them whip all the run out you. I don't want to go that way. (150)[17]

It is a lesson that Wideman himself has learned. In fact, Wideman uses the novel to confront the fundamental part of his problem: running away. Physically, by running to Wyoming, and mentally, by writing from a Eurocentric perspective, Wideman has been hiding out. With the writing of *Hiding Place,* Wideman has made a qualitative leap toward his Africanness, for he writes about the inability of people—Tommy, Bess, and himself—to run away from their problems. Thus, Tommy's words about himself are really Wideman's own self-appraisal:

> I was scared a long time. Ever since my granddaddy John French died and his house fell to pieces and everybody scattered I been scare. Scared of people, scared of myself. Of how I look and how I talk, of the nigger in me. Scared of what people said about me. But I got no time to be scared now. Ain't no reason to be scared now cause ain't nothing they can take from me now. (151)

Acceptance brings commitment. By the end of the novel, Tommy commits himself to confront the criminal charges against him; Bess commits herself to speak up in Tommy's behalf ("Because somebody has to go down there and tell the truth" [158]); Wideman commits himself to mingle with his people and to write the truth about them.[18] Just as Tommy and Bess come down from Bruston Hill, Wideman comes down from his high horse (i.e., the pole that Cecil's Uncle Otis refers to in *Hurry Home*) to be a part of his people. In this regard, the last line in the novel can be seen as Wideman's speaking directly to the reader about himself: "She's coming to tell them he ain't scared no more and they better listen and they better make sure it don't happen so easy ever again" (158). The prodigal son returns home.

After *Hiding Place,* Wideman is able to talk about himself more frankly. Indirect references in that novel change to direct ones in his next two. With acceptance comes full examination. The second

work in the Homewood Trilogy, *Damballah* opens with an introduction in which Wideman speaks directly to his incarcerated
brother, Robby (the Tommy of *Hiding Place*), for it is his brother,
and all those other family members (race members—female and
male—will be included in this family in later works) reflected in
and through Robby, who helps shape Wideman's consciousness of
himself as an African:

> He has seen his brother cry once before. Doesn't want to see it again.
> Too many faces in his brother's face. Starting with their mother and
> going back and going sideways and all of Homewood there if he
> looked long enough. Not just faces but streets and stories and rooms
> and songs. ("Tommy" 174)[19]

In fact, the book is dedicated "To Robby":

> Consider all these stories as letters from home. I never liked water-
> melon as a kid. I think I remember you did. You weren't afraid of
> becoming instant nigger, of sitting barefoot and goggle-eyes and Day-
> Glo black and drippy-lipped on massa's fence if you took one bit of
> the forbidden fruit. I was too scared to enjoy watermelon. Too self-
> conscious. I let people rob me of a simple pleasure.

In admitting that he let others define him, to rob him of his
African centeredness, Wideman shows just how much he is committed to self-scrutiny, no matter how painful the process and
no matter what the consequences. It is a self-examination that is
sparked by juxtaposing his life with that of his brother. To understand his brother's life choices, he has to understand his own. For
instance, Why he was the acclaimed author (one of the "one of a
kinds") instead of the incarcerated brother(s). What he discovers
is shocking, earth-shattering knowledge of his own weaknesses,
for it is he who is the one who shames the family the most. Robby
runs away from the police after committing a crime that almost
seems inevitable for those African men like Robby who struggle
to hold on to their identity (i.e., their manness). Wideman runs
away from his roots, his community, his family, himself after committing a crime far worse than armed robbery, the crime of self-
hatred, African hatred. Coleman agrees:

> In some ways, little has changed between the times of Sybella [Wide-
> man's great, great grandmother] and Tommy, but they had the nerve

to run away, to rebel against slavery and the roles prescribed for them. The narrator ran away also, but his running was no rebellion and set no example for others. Before living life in the community where he really interacted with and influenced others, the narrator slipped away through a kind of intellectual and literary passing that benefited only him.[20]

Like the Jupiter Hammon that makes the best of himself within an exploitive, oppressive slave environment, seemingly unmindful of his fellow slaves, Wideman prostitutes himself at a time, the 1960s, when his brothers and sisters are sacrificing, rebelling against a system that exploits all African people. Wideman kills his African self, not just by refusing to struggle for the collective, but also by refusing to struggle for his own identity. Instead, he escapes—both in theory (his writings, especially his first two novels) and in practice (his marriage to Judy, his life in Wyoming, far removed from Homewood). His choices are those of Cecil in *Hurry Home*. Choice One: Be with the African masses and let them "drag you down, eat you up." Choice Two: "You—you are one of a kind. You will be treated accordingly." Like Cecil, Wideman opts for "Choice two, choice two is unavoidable. Everyone likes to be thought of as unique don't they. One of a kind, treated accordingly" (153–54).

Damballah too is significant in that it documents Wideman's growth from the examination of his own personal family roots to community, cultural roots. To choose "Damballah" as the first story, a story that reflects the roots of a people in Africa, and then to choose the name of that story as the title of the whole collection of short stories reflect Wideman's increasing consciousness of himself as an African. "Damballah" celebrates African history by reclaiming the African in African-American literature. The main character is Orion who, in finding his Africanness, accepts the responsibility of passing on the precious history of African people so that neither the people, nor the culture is ever destroyed:

Damballah said it be a long way a ghost be going and Jordan chilly and wide and a new ghost take his time getting his wings together. Long way to go so you can't sit and listen till the ghost ready to go home. The boy wiped his wet hands on his knees and drew the cross and said the word and settled down and listened to Orion tell the stories again. Orion talked and he listened and couldn't stop listening till he saw Orion's eyes rise up through the back of the severed skull and lips rise up through the skull and the wings of the ghost measure out the rhythm of one last word. (25)

Wideman too has discovered his history, his roots, has accepted them and commits himself to share. It is an acceptance and commitment that brings extraordinary powers. Because, as Wideman has learned, immersing oneself in his culture gives him millions of eyes in which to see, hands with which to feel and write, feet with which to travel, mouths with which to taste and communicate, ears with which to hear and learn. Empowers one, in the spirit of Damballah, to "Gather up the Family."

Damballah then is the first work in which Wideman fully and clearly examines himself. It is a painful process, the recognition that you betrayed your own, but what's even more painful is *admitting* that you have done it. In "The Chinaman," Wideman comes to terms with his tendency to run away by admitting it to all of his readers: "I was glad I was far away and didn't have to trek to the hospital [when his grandmother was sick]. But the others were faithful" (93). While painful, self-analysis is also fulfilling, rewarding, humbling, and admirable. Knowing full well that everyone makes mistakes, the people always admire those who admit them and move on with their lives. *Damballah*, therefore, is also "a moving on" work. Once Wideman discovers his mistakes, then admits them, he wastes no time in getting on, or getting down, with the next order of business: the celebration of his roots.

So, in "The Chinaman," he celebrates those family members who stood steadfast while he abandoned ship when his grandmother Freeda was hospitalized. In "The Beginning of Homewood," Wideman celebrates both Tommy, i.e., his brother Robby, and Sybela Owens, his ancestor who came to Homewood in 1859:

What was not simple was my need to tell Sybela's story so it connected with yours [Tommy's/Robby's]. One was root and the other branch but I was too close to you and she was too far away and there was the matter of guilt, of responsibility. I couldn't tell either story without implicating myself. (195)

In "The Songs of Reba Love Jackson," Wideman celebrates the African community, its victimization, its struggle to heal itself through song, its overall blackness. Indeed, in the story, the image of life is Blackness; that of death is white: "White hands were peeling away his skin. White eyes lay on him like a blanket of snow. White feet stomped on his chest. . . . he was too cold to be dead. He was someplace where white people were talking and laughing" (127). In "Watermelon Man," Wideman struggles to fuse together all people of African descent, all places of African descent, by refusing to see any clear, important distinctions among them: "It was Africa you see. Or Georgy or someplace back there. It don't make no difference no way. Niggers be niggers anyplace they be. If you get my meaning" (103).

Sent for You Yesterday is the last work in the Homewood trilogy. It is the one that brings together into one whole all the pieces of Wideman's family history to show the connection between and within generations as well as the responsibilities each generation has to fulfill. The inscription of the novel clarifies this traditional African communal message of oneness: "Past lives live in us, through us. Each of us harbors the spirits of people who walked the earth before we did, and those spirits depend on us for continuing existence, just as we depend on their presence to live our lives to the fullest."[21] It is a oneness, an interconnectedness that brings with it responsibility just as it did within the African communal context. Also, it is a oneness that is rooted in Africanness, no matter how that African looks or how that African acts. The message that's most important is that together we're somebody; apart we're nobody. I am my brother's keeper.

It is significant then that one of the main characters is Brother Tate who is totally in tuned with the community despite the fact that he is an albino—the whitest of Africans, and despite the fact that he communicates with sounds, musical sounds, not words. Of his skin color, Wideman writes that Brother's whiteness "made him less nigger and more nigger at the same time" (17) and his whiteness was a hated color, yet he was "nigger, the blackest, purest kind stamped his features. The thick lips, the broad flaring wings of his nose" (131). What's most important is Brother's concern for and immersion in the African community, a rootedness that makes him seem older and wiser than most of the characters in the novel: "He was just a boy but sometimes he seemed older than [Freeda] was. Sometimes he was older than old Mr. and Mrs. Tate who they say had found him and raised him" (38).[22]

This rootedness in Africanness that the albino has despite his physical appearance and verbal handicap is one Wideman must come to terms with in this novel. It is a rootedness that Wideman now sees himself connected to since he, in his early adult life, assumed a white lifestyle (i.e., was an albino) and communicated little, if at all, with other Africans, especially in his literary works. It is a rootedness or sense of oneness that also comes from knowledge, respect, and love—elements that Wideman seem not to have inherited or learned to appreciate from his family. In fact, the John French family, as seen in earlier novels and in this one, set themselves apart from and even ridicule the African community. Perhaps the two people whom Wideman most respected as a child were his grandmother Freeda and grandfather John French. And it is these two people who seem the most exacting critics of the race. For example, it is the poor struggling Homewood Africans that Freeda blames for the oppression of the community, not capitalism, nor even the Pittsburgh or Pennsylvania authorities:

> She hated the fat, buzzing flies. Flies in Cassina Way had never been bad till all those people from the deep South started arriving with their dirty boxes and bags and spitting in the street and throwing garbage where people have to walk. It was like having all those people in her house when the flies swarmed through the open door, those careless, dirty people lighting on her things, crawling across her ceilings and floors. (35)

Hers is clearly a Euro-centered view of the poor African community, a view which sees the victim as the criminal and surely a view which Europeans had of Sybela Owens, Freeda's own ancestor, when she first came to Homewood. It is a Euro-centered view that is passed on to Wideman himself so that he has to grow to understand not to be ashamed of poverty, but to hold the perpetuators accountable:

> You could see that stretch of Cassina from Susquehanna after the city urban renewed Homewood. Our old house still standing then next to the vacant lot. A row of wooden shanties anchored in rubble, so thin and old and exposed they shamed me and I looked away quickly, the way I averted my eyes from the crotches of ancient women in head rags and cotton stockings rolled to their knees who sat gap-legged on their porches. (23)

And he does learn to blame the victimizer, to stop seeing African children as "burr-head," their mamas, roaches who flee "every which way from the cracks and crevices where they hide at night" (41); the grandmothers ("ancient women") as "wooden shanties anchored in rubble, so thin and old and exposed they shamed me." Instead, those to blame are "the ones who ran Homewood without ever setting foot in Homewood. The ones whose lily-white hands held Homewood like a lemon and squeezed pennies out drop by drop and every drop bitter as tears, sour as sweat when you work all day and ain't got nothing to show for it" (80). It is the manipulators of Homewood who make the victims hate themselves, make them believe that "crossing t's and dotting i's had something to do with becoming a human being and blackness was the chaos you had to learn to whip into shape in order to be a person who counted" (135).

Wideman's understanding of the oneness that does and must exist among African people (race-nation perspective) and his understanding of his people's position in society in connection to the means of production (class perspective) empowers him to see that it is never too late for the individual to return to the collective whole; that it is never too late to assume a socially responsible role in connection to that whole. That is, this the third novel in the Homewood Trilogy is important in showing Wideman his integral connection to and role in the African community. The title, "Sent for you Yesterday," makes sense in this connection. From the Count Basie/Jimmy Rushing classic, "Sent for you yesterday, here you come today, but you're right on time," the title has significance on several levels. First, things past—even twenty-five years or more—seem like yesterday when you are involved in, relate to, and are proud of your history. Second, you can never run from the past as Wideman tried to do because you always run right back to the source: "Just a circle going round and round so you getting closer while you getting further away and further while you getting closer" (118). Third, it's never too late to return to the fold, one's family, community, nation. When you do, you're still right on time. It is the source—the history, the nation, the people—that nurture you; props you up and gives you direction so that you can stand on your own. Thus, it is significant that Wideman first learns to dance while listening to "Sent for You." Lucy gets him up on his feet and moving; then Wideman's on his own:

She pulled you on your feet and started swaying you to the music, side to side, but you jerked away. Wanted to do your own thing. She got you moving but she had to turn you loose. . . .Hardly big as a minute and out there dancing by yourself. Count Basie playing with Jimmy Rushing on vocal. (118–19)

After learning that it is never too late to return to the community and assume a socially responsible role within it, Wideman must determine what this role can be based on his skills. Of course, it is writing, what he has always been doing, but writing now defined by one's Africanness, a perspective that not only presents historically accurate information in terms of the victim and the victimizer, but also one which struggles to propose solutions for the victim's dilemma. And since the victim is the African, since all Africans are connected, since all experience a similar oppression, they can tell each other's story. Being both brothers and keepers (sisters and brothers, sisters and keepers), Lucy can tell Samantha's story; Brother can tell Wilkes' story; Wideman can tell our story. Being both brothers and keepers (sisters and brothers, sisters and keepers), Uncle Carl can begin Brother's story and Lucy can end it; Wideman can begin the African's story, and some other African writer can end it.

For Wideman, the first solution is to protest, to speak out against the victimization. It is within this context that Brother's train dream makes sense.

Serving not only as introduction to, but also framework for the novel, Brother's dream presents the victimization of the African and proposes the only two solutions that the victim has in this society: to remain silent and accept one's exploitation and oppression or to speak out and risk one's life:

Arms and legs and pieces of people slamming all up against you and nobody saying s'cuse me or sorry. People just rolling around like marbles on the floor of that boxcar. Quiet as lambs cept every once in a while all the sudden you hear somebody scream. Ain't no doors nor windows but you know they gone. Nobody left after a scream like that. . . . I knew if I'da screamed I'd be gone. If I scream I'd be like them other poor suckers screaming and flying away. That scream would take me with it. My insides. And all my outsides too. So I didn't scream. (10)

To scream is to risk death, literally and figuratively. Figuratively, Wideman could risk his writing career. But it is a risk he takes, for from now on Wideman will speak out, not just about his biological brother's victimization, but, as the African nation's brother and keeper, he will protest the victimization of all his people. It is a qualitative leap for Wideman because he no longer allows the society to define him (e.g., Thurley and Webb as definers), nor does he allow himself to wobble in ambivalence about who he is. Instead, feeling assured of his identity, he will explore all facets of Africanness. Dance within himself. Burst the boundaries of fiction from an African-centered perspective. Thus, the last line of the novel aptly describes Wideman's writing stages: "I'm on my own feet. Learning to stand, to walk, learning to dance."

With the writing of *Reuben*, Wideman is certainly dancing, having found a centeredness, a balance from within African culture. No longer merely interested in family roots, in this work, Wideman explores the role he can play within the community, always with the eye of one who is centered. This eye/I is at odds with the one shaped by his family background, because it is an eye/I that sees itself within, not without the people and the culture. Unlike *Sent for You Yesterday* then, the masses of Africans are not roaches scrambling out of a lighted oven, but people living in rat-like conditions. It is not the people who are the problem, but the oppressive, economic conditions. It is the oven that turns the people into roaches, the garbage can dwellings that turn them into rats:

> Laid out naked to the world behind some garbage cans, her mouth open, her thighs open, alley dirt and alley filth and she's stretched out in it dead as a stick . . . Kwansa heard the story like everybody else and clucked her tongue and wondered about the children who found the dead girl, wondered why some mother had struggled to give the girl life, carried her, nursed her, squeezed her bleeding into the world and what would that mother think if she saw her daughter like those boys found her? A baby once. A little sweet baby once. Like us all. . . . These streets and alleys, these trifling chicken-coop houses close in on you like a rat in a trap. (138–39)[23]

We're all born sweet little babies, but oppressive conditions—shacks that burn down every winter, older people who are found in boarded-up shacks only after their bodies begin to stink, shacks "no self-respecting roach call home"—change us (142). Graveyards make us niggers; Africans don't make environments graveyards. These negative conditions impact upon the whole race, children, women, and men. African men, with good intentions, turn into wanted men, runaway fathers who don't support their children:

> Kwansa's seen the young men rise in the morning, shaved, hair combed, a pressed company shirt, rise with that serious look and go down the hill like clockwork when she was living with her Big Mama on Tokay. . . . For months rain or shine you could set your clock by them passing Big Mama's window on their way to meet the man. Then they'd fall. Start missing days. Falter and fall. Their eyes went first. (145)

In placing the blame primarily on society, not primarily on the men, Wideman is once again looking at the impact objective conditions have on African people. It is a shift in point of view, a view conditioned by how you see yourself (identity) and your level of understanding of yourself in connection with the rest of the world (history). Being within African culture, Wideman sees the importance of African traditions and institutions that, as an outsider, he once devalued. For example, the African church, ridiculed in Wideman's early works, is praised in *Reuben* as an institution that offers stabilization, energy, collectivism, and hope to the African community. Wideman has a new respect for it, a new understanding of its value as earthly healer, and a new recognition of the overall positive role it plays in the community:

> There is no song louder than the troubles in your heart so you hum till the hum is echoed by another and another and rather than die, rather than split apart on these squealing folding chairs advertising funeral parlors, you let the other voices take you, ease your burden, let them carry your cry because you are lifting theirs in the chorus of some old anthem everybody knows. (150–51)

Compare this newfound respect for the corner church in the African community with Wideman's negative appraisal in *A Glance Away*, one filtered through Daddy Eugene's eyes. The church is ridiculed; the African God, a buffoon with shining teeth:

Tioga Street Sanctified in the Name of Jesus Christ Church said glassed
over scroll in homemade gold letters on black cardboard. Two large
windows, that on hot days had to be opened faced DaddyGene and
me on our perch. Almost like being inside from where we sat. . . .
Like mourners all were dressed in black, white shirts of men crackling
in contrast beneath dark heads and necks, women's hair cropped and
netted or veiled so each had a black, fat bag atop her head. . . . Inside
nothing but the shouting and chanting of the voice next to you could
be heard. Let the King of Glory come in. And he did in top hat and
tie, wearing striped pants and immaculate white, gold-buttoned spats
on shining shoes. His teeth glinted brighter than diamond stickpin or
rings big as quarters on his fingers, a slender, silver-tipped cane
winked as it whirled enchanted in the air. Won't you come home Bill
Bailey, won't you come home. Who is the King of Glory. Your host
baby, your toastmaster, and number one promoter of the biggest scene
going. And they hallelujahed and wept and laughed with joy, shaking
their heads—um um—eyes aglow. (13–14, 15)

Wideman does not just move from a worldwide perspective held
by Europeans, but a European-centered perspective held by anyone, including miseducated Africans like Daddy Eugene. It is a
perspective of the world that sees events and people through the
eyes of one who sees Europe and its people at the center of the
universe, and all those other events and people as aberrations of
Europe. For Africans, it is a petty bourgeois view, a view that is
actuated and perpetuated as a result of self-hatred, a view that
has been conditioned by the education and propaganda of a
European-dominated world. It is the view of Wideman's family.
    Having explored his family roots in the Homewood Trilogy,
understood its positive life-saving values and its negative people-
killing elements, Wideman in *Reuben* takes the painful step of
cutting the umbilical cord. If centered in Africanness, Wideman
must divorce his view of and relationship to the community from
those of Grandma Freeda and DaddyGene. And just as Wideman's
understanding of the dialectical relationship between the objective
conditions and subjective reality of the community has increased
so has his understanding of the necessity of practical, not just
theoretical endeavors, in bringing about a change in this community. Therefore, the protagonist in *Reuben* is one who has dedicated himself to helping poor, struggling Africans in Homewood:
"Turns out I'm a sort of go-between. I stand between my clients

and their problems. I intercede, let them step aside awhile. I take the weight. For a while at least ease a bit of their burden. . . . Mostly I listen" (198). Assuming a role of savior, similar to that of Christ, certainly comparable to a tzaddik (Reuben literally means, "Behold, a son" [127]), Reuben dedicates himself to what he considers the best class of people, poor Africans like Kwansa who have no one else to turn to: "Deal with a better class of people now. Our people, Wally. Homewood people. The best" (197).[24] Of course, just as Reuben works for a better class, the struggling African masses, so Wideman writes for a better class, the African masses, since his subject is now them, not the intellectual, petty bourgeoisie or the European who sees the world as beginning and ending with him (and I mean *him*).

And as an African hero, not a European hero, Reuben is not depicted as a man larger than life, a Tall Paul Bunyan of heroic stature, but a small, unassuming man whose great commitment is based on his recognition of the needs of his people. His dedication is commiserate with his level of consciousness about his people's suffering, not with his physical appearance. So it is the mind, the head of Reuben, that is big; the body has been dwarfed by capitalism:

> Reuben was a small man. His face was long and his hands long, but Reuben never grew taller than the average twelve-year-old boy. That long head atop a puny body, the way he carried one shoulder higher than the other, reminded people how close Reuben had come to being a hunchbacked dwarf. . . . the face narrowed drastically, coming to a sharp point at his chin, a point, some said, sharp enough to bust balloons or prick your finger. (1–2)

Reuben is the Littleman of *The Lynchers,* but with a clearer, more practical understanding of his relationship to the community. From the first page of the novel, Reuben (and by association, Wideman) is established as a conscious person. He is Wideman's first protagonist who is both equipped to and who does help the African community. Unlike either Littleman or Wilkerson, Reuben's commitment is based on his understanding of his relationship to family, community, and nation rather than on an artificial, unrealistic commitment based on ignorance. (Littleman has no family and Wilkerson is not committed to the plan.)

Reuben's life work, living quarters, and office are clear reflec-

tions of his commitment. Not only does he live with the community, instead of without (in the suburbs or in Wyoming), but he
lives all around it. His home is a trailer, giving him the potential
to literally go where the people are: "You need Reuben here he
come like a turtle or some damned something his whole house
dragging behind him. On Saturdays he'd have that contraption
packed up on Homewood Avenue. And people be in and out all
day like ants after honey" (6).

What Wideman comes to understand, however, is that Reuben
cannot do it all alone. Admirable as he is, Reuben—one individual—cannot take on the weight of the problems of the race. Over-
burdened and overworked, Reuben experiences burn-out. He
begins to doubt his own ability to help ("For her [Kwansa's] sake
he'd play the game. Trek downtown. Pretend he could change her
story" [47]). He begins to hear voices, all the voices of the oppressed Africans who want, no need, his help ("Lately, his memory
had become more like those all night, call-in, radio talk shows, an
unpredictable mix of voices coming from anywhere and nowhere,
voices with nothing in common but an 800 number that gave them
access to a private space within him" [6]). He begins to move less
and less around the community ("To see Reuben now you got to
go to him," [6]), and, thus, he begins to rely on mysticism—magic,
charms, and voodoo:

> A rag, a bone, a hank of hair. Ancient grains of rice, feathers, stones,
> a plastic baggie of grave dirt, a string of jingle bells, leaves, dried
> insects, pebbles of colored glass, seashells, bits of broken mirror,
> needles and thread, more stones. . . . Then he gathered a little bit of
> this, a little bit of that from the box, carefully folding each item he
> harvested into his own compartment in the length of cloth. . . . Reu-
> ben braids them together, parent and child. (69–71)[25]

Reuben and Wideman need help. Though both recognize the
necessity of practical action in changing objective conditions—that
by changing these conditions, one changes the subjective reality of
African people, neither has the power to make decisive changes
alone. In *Philadelphia Fire,* Wideman's next work, Wideman will
move one step closer to evolving a solution—entreating his audience to aid in this problem-solving process. *Reuben* does not reflect
this level of understanding, but it does reflect Wideman's awareness of the need for more—more than mere writing about the

problem (African people need action) and more than one person's commitment (African people need the energy of the collective): "And the truth seems less than enough. It won't set us free. We need more. Truth just starts the wheels turning. There's more . . . we need more than truth to save us now" (201).

Philadelphia Fire has three principal, interwoven thematic threads. First, framing the novel is the factual story of the bombing of the MOVE house on Osage Avenue in Philadelphia (13 May 1985) on the orders of Mayor Wilson Goode.[26] Second, the novel is about father-son relationships: Cudjoe's (the name is a derivative of the west African name, "Kojo," meaning unconquerable) and Simba's, Prospero's (a prosperous capitalist) and Caliban's (*American Heritage Dictionary*, 1981: "In Shakespeare *Tempest*, the grotesque, brutish slave . . . Perhaps alteration of Cariban, from Cariban *caribe*, "brave"), and Wideman's and his imprisoned son's. Thus, the title describes not only the physical occurrence on Osage, but also Cudjoe's and Wideman's personal fire (baptism) as well as the African nation's fire that resulted from the *mfekane* (the slave trade, slavery, and colonization and the consequences of these experiences) of which the Prospero-Caliban section of the novel symbolizes. Third, the novel is about Wideman's own fire. It is his most personal novel to date, one in which he reappraises his life, discovers how "fucked up" it was/is, and nearly commits suicide. All in all, in this novel Wideman is very much conscious of the connection among people, events, and time periods. So the image of fire significantly reverberates throughout the novel, smelting together disparate elements, destroying, cleansing, and creating anew. MOVE's hell is our hell. That's one message. Another is, "If the shoe fits, wear it."

Structurally, the novel is divided into three logical parts: The first concerns the protagonist Cudjoe and his search for Simba, a MOVE child who escapes the fire physically unharmed, but mentally scarred for life. The second part concerns Wideman and his relationship with his imprisoned (i.e., lost) son. The third concerns the colonial father's (i.e., Prospero's) relationship with the colonized, or "lost" children (i.e., Caliban). Increasingly, however, it becomes clear that it is the fathers who are lost (mentally lost), not the children. Thus, the world of the novel is topsy-turvy. The fathers, because they act like children, are the children; the children are the parents. It is the fathers who have run away from their homes; they are the runagates in need of finding (that is, discovering) themselves.

Having forsaked his wife and children, Cudjoe, when the novel opens, is lost on a Greek island, seven thousand miles away from Philadelphia, living in a crystal ball, letting "nothing outside the sealed ball [touch] what's inside. Hermetic. Unreachable. Locked in" (5).[27] (How appropriate the setting: Greece—the citadel of western civilization!) It is the MOVE bombing which explodes the ball, which precipitates Cudjoe's return to Philadelphia though he had been long haunted by images of Greek children whose skinny, dark bodies (a reminder of African children?) he had to step over to negotiate his way to and from the beach. But it is the MOVE fire that moves him from the level of thought to action. His first act, on his return, is to interview a MOVE survivor, Margaret Jones. It is through Cudjoe's initial conversations with her that Wideman explores the two, disparate, unreconcilable visions of the Euro-centered and the African-centered. That is, Wideman uses this, his most recent novel, to examine the principal contradiction in his life.

Like Wideman, Margaret Jones first viewed the African masses from a Euro-centered perspective, her initial impression of King, the leader of MOVE, being "a trifling dreadlocked man draped back wriggling his bare toes. . . . I know it ain't just him stinking up the whole neighborhood. It's the house behind him, the tribe of crazy people in it" (12). Then she, like Wideman, begins to analyze what it means to be African in the U.S.:

> Things spozed to get better, ain't they? Somewhere down the line, it ought to get better or what's the point scuffling like we do? Don't have to squat in weeds and wipe my behind with a leaf. Running water inside my house and in the supermarket I can buy thirty kinds of soda pop, twelve different colors of toilet paper. But that ain't what I call progress. Do you? (14)

Margaret's move from a European-centered perspective to an African-centered one allows her to re-evaluate King and people like him:

> King said out loud what I been knowing all along. Newspapers said King brainwashing and mind control and drugs and kidnapping peo-

ple turn them to zombies. Bullshit. . . . By then stink wasn't really stink no more. Just confusion. A confused idea. An idea from outside the family, outside the teachings causing me to turn my nose up at my own natural self. (15)

Margaret's nation-class analysis (seeing herself as African and poor) of African people helps Cudjoe to see himself more clearly, to see that he too viewed the world by standing in the shadow of the European, lost in otherness. But now he is found. Now his perspective is African centered: "He'll tell Margaret Jones we're all in this together. That he was lost but now he's found" (22).

Now "saved," Cudjoe/Wideman is equipped to see the world as it really is for most Africans, to see that the one sector most impacted upon by capitalism is the youth, not just Simba, but "every black boy I've ever seen" (94), including Wideman's own son. Indeed, understanding the collective plight of the African youth allows Cudjoe/Wideman to replace his search for one lost boy, Simba, for a lost generation, or for a lost people with one for a solution. Thus Part Two of *Philadelphia Fire* begins with Wideman's own story about his wife Judy and their sons and ends with the colonization of the African by the Great White Father as represented by Prospero. And, dialectically, by reviewing the history of the exploitation and oppression of the collective, Wideman better understands himself and his son; Cudjoe is better able to understand that there are thousands of Simbas who are lost (Kaliban Kiddie Korps) and thousands of Calibans who are lost. So the objective is not to find or save one, but to save all.

Learning more about the exploited sons and the lost fathers result in a qualitative leap in Wideman's consciousness about himself. In realizing he knew "next to nothing about" his son, the youth, the race, he breaks down, at first blaming himself instead of the society: "And here he was responsible. Knowing no other god. No good reason not to rip the wheel off the steering post" (22). This "nervous breakdown" in turn impacts upon his ability to write: "But it was so hard to write. I'd get an idea. . . . But before I could manage to write it down, it was gone" (107). But once Wideman puts the pieces together— the MOVE story, his story, the colonized's story, the African's story, he correctly places the blame where it belongs, capitalist U.S.A.: "Some of us, a few really, are doing better, moving up. A handful doing damned well.

But them that ain't got and never had, they worse off than ever. S.O.S., man. Rich richer and poor poorer" (79). The next step for Wideman then is to discover how the exploitation began and to relate it to the present, to put these pieces together. This quilting he does and does well through Cudjoe's street version of the historical relevance of Shakespeare and his tales, specifically *The Tempest*:

> Yes, Willy was now. Peeped the hole card [the slave trade and colonization]. Scoped the whole ugly mess about to happen at that day and time which brings us to here, to today. To this very moment in our contemporary world. To the inadequacy of your background, your culture. Its inability, like the inability of a dead sea, to cast up on the beach appropriate models, creatures whose lives you might imitate. (128)

As his own self-appraisal makes clear, Wideman certainly was taught the Willy lesson well; and lived to imitate the great master:

> Why he swoop down like great god from the sky, try make everybody feel high? Take ebryting. Den ebryting give back. Go off teach at University. Write book. Host talk show. Jah self don't know what next dis dicty gentleman do. (121)

Both Cudjoe and Wideman heal themselves by self-analysis ushered in by race and individual catastrophes. Through their appraisals, both learn three useful lessons: that running away from the problem solves nothing; that the individual African's dilemma is reflective of that of the race; and that the solution to the individual's plight is the salvation of the collective. How those useful lessons work out in the novel is easy to explain. First, Cudjoe steels himself to face his enemy, not to run away, no matter how overwhelming the odds seem:

> Cudjoe hears footsteps behind him. A mob howling his name. Screaming for blood. Words come to him, cool him, stop him in his tracks. He'd known them all his life. *Never again. Never again.* He turns to face whatever it is rumbling over the stones of Independence Square. (199)

Second, Cudjoe abandons his search for Simba by the end of the novel; instead, he engages in a collective commemorative ceremony for all the victims of MOVE, for himself, and the race: "A hot day like this, my soul brothers. And here you are again making no connections, taking out no insuracne. C'mon. Follow me. Before they decide to sweep your corner clean" (193). Third, while neither Cudjoe nor Wideman seem to fully understand the nature of the problem or its only permanent solution, they do know that theory without practice is empty. Action is needed: "Better to light one little candle than to sit on one's ass and write clever, irresponsible, fanciful accounts of what never happened, never will. Lend a hand" (157).

Writing is not enough, Wideman learns. We must get off our individual corners and do something, otherwise, who knows, "Perhaps you will be consumed by the fire."

3

"And Arn't I a Woman": Wideman's Women

There are elements within the Wideman canon that serve as gauges of the author's gradual centering of himself within the African world and his corresponding de-centering of himself from the European world. One of these gauges is his treatment of women. While this treatment never becomes progressive enough to allow him to focus extensively and expressly on his own relationship with his European wife, Judy, it does allow him to allude to her and to imply a set of circumstances which reflects his growing African-centeredness. Of course, his least conscious treatment of women appears early in the canon; his most conscious, in *Philadelphia Fire*.

In 1852 Sojourner Truth stood before a mostly hostile, predominantly European audience at a Woman's Rights Convention in Akron, Ohio and questioned the accepted notions of African-hood, womanhood, and labor-hood. Her speech, entitled "And Arn't I a Woman," forced the audience to view women who are African and those who work as hard as men as just as much an example of womanhood as those who sit fanning themselves on the veranda:

Well, chillun, whar dar is so much racket, dar must be something out o' kilter. I t'ink dat 'twizt de niggers of de Souf an' de women at de Norf' all a talkin' bout rights, de white men will be in a fix pretty soon. But what's all dis here talkin' about? Dat man ober dar say dat women needs to be helped into carriages, and lifted ober ditches, and to have de best place everywhere. . . . Nobody eber helped me into carriages, or ober mud puddles, or give me any best place! And arn't I a Woman? Look at me. Look at my arm. I have plowed and planted and tathered into barns and no man could head me—and arn't I a woman? I have born'd five chilrun and seen 'em mos' all sold off into slavery, and when I cried out with mother's grief, none but Jesus heard . . . and arn't I a woman?[1]

Despite the nearly century and a half since Truth's speech, the popular standards of womanhood have remained those of the slave era. Real women are slim and fragile; real women are beautiful only if they have long hair, light eyes, and keen features. Real women are wealthy. Real women are European women. Determined by the ruling capitalist class, these stereotypes of the woman are still accepted by the unquestioned mind, both European and African. Perhaps what is most unfortunate is that Africans such as Wideman have embraced these notions despite the fact that the acceptance of such race, class, gender standards are genocidal for African people.

Wideman's early works generally characterize the African woman as ugly or, if not, cold. Women, both European and African, are important as physical objects of beauty (if they are European or European-like) and/or mates to husbands, having no real identity of their own. Wideman's second writing stage is marked by his concentration on African women within his family. Still, these women all possess European physical traits, and their greatest contribution to humanity is child (and husband) rearing. In *Reuben* and *Philadelphia Fire,* the works which mark the third and final writing stage thus far, Wideman presents struggling African women with typically African characteristics. For example, the presentation of Kwansa (i.e., Kwanzaa, the African-American celebration) in *Reuben* is one which reveals that Wideman is looking at the world through the eyes of the African woman. Then too he presents, for the first time, the African lesbian's point of view, a view that has been conditioned by an inner city environment. In *Philadelphia Fire* Wideman looks at women from a personal perspective in that he alludes to his relationship with his wife. Although the woman appears only in connection to the three central men—Cudjoe, Caliban, and Wideman, the woman is of European descent and has been intentionally planted by the prosperous capitalist (i.e., Prospero) to seduce the unwitting African male.

All the women in *A Glance Away* are flat and negatively portrayed, though still able to attract the African male. The first portrait of the European woman is of one who is a selfish, whorish,

racist vampire, sucking the life blood of men. When Eddie is re-
leased from a drug detoxification center in the South, he meets
a European woman on the bus he boards for home and sums her
up as "a woman, unattractive, even repulsive behind thick round
spectacle whose slightest whim, whose pleasure or displeasure was
worth his life" (25). Clara, the European friend of Eddie's ex-
girlfriend Alice, proves her belief in equality by having sex with
Eddie. Our overall impression of her can be summed up as a
negative aftertaste, the same as Eddie's: "White Clara naked on
his bed. He had been so confused, so tender, and afterwards the
pasty, sour smell of her sex wouldn't leave his fingers" (25). Yet,
clearly, Eddie was sufficiently attracted to Clara to have sex with
her. The European woman, then, is both physically attractive, yet
selfish and destructive. For example, Thurley's wife and his
mother both dominate and manipulate him to such an extent that
they beat him into homosexuality. It is the woman who is portrayed as the enemy of men, not the economic system of capitalism
which beats men into boys.

Wideman's portrayal of African women is not positively drawn
either. Those related to the protagonist have some European features, what Wideman calls, "fine and fair," but have no life outside
their men. After the death of her husband, Eddie's own mother
stopped walking and cursed her God (29). A cold, grasping, bitter
woman, she wants Eddie to herself, altogether ignoring or verbally
abusing his best friend, Brother, and seeing her own daughter,
who sacrifices her life for her mother, as a whore (55). Her family,
specifically the men in the family, is her life. So when the other
men in her life are dead, Eddie becomes all: son, brother, even
lover:

> She started into the open doorway still blinking from the sudden
> burst of light. Over her shoulders long gray-brown braids hung down
> like little girls'. The dingy flannel nightdress had come open at the
> throat, and as she slowly twisted, for an instant the sun high-lighted
> the hollow and curve of her neck making the skin soft and smooth
> again. Through the doorway her lover would return; she bit her lip
> to make it stop trembling, to assume a smile or frown because Eddie
> was home. (54)

Altogether Wideman's early women—whether European or African—live because the men give them life. No matter their hard-

ships, they have been rewarded in life because they have interacted with men: "Life had touched his [Eddie's] mother, made her old too soon. But there had been other things for her. She had been wife, mother, her years had been full" (123). Wideman's lack of consciousness about the plight of women is a reflection of his early, superficial writing, seeing from without, using the eyes of a European male conditioned by capitalism. It is a reflection of that immature thinking that makes some men view women as an extension of themselves: "I asked her if she needed my eyes too, so much to see she smiled and closed both hers saying no you take mine and tell me what we see" (*Hurry* 131).

In *Hurry Home* Wideman's belief that to be as much like the European, or better still, to be a European is to be the most beautiful woman dominates: "So much red on the pillow, soft red he can smooth or tangle in his fist. He should be brave. The flesh of her he can bathe in as he pleases. The sleep-snow whiteness in which he can ink deeply the heat of his hands, foot or lips" (7). It is almost a nauseating reflection of Wideman's early Eurocentric perspective, so far is he removed from seeing beauty in "blackness." Added to this love of European women is the idea that they are more intelligent than African women, for Esther, the only African female in the novel, is not only depicted as ugly, but also ignorant, having eyes that are "dog eyes, cow eyes, baleful, uncomprehending" (6). This is the view of Cecil, the protagonist of the novel whom Esther sacrifices her life for by working extra jobs to put him through law school:

> I always thought of my reward in terms of Cecil's success, in the maturing of my love whether it was returned or not. I asked no promises. I lived with him as helpmate, as wife, never asking more than the knowledge in my soul that I was achieving Your appointed task, though my duty took me along darksome, unfrequented paths. (127)

Yet for all of her sacrifices, Cecil sees her as stupid and ugly, repaying her by taking her money, moving out of their bed, and running away. On one occasion, he even negatively contrasts her vagina hair with that of a European: "Esther's was a hedge you had to crawl through before the meadow spread sunlit and swaying, but these feathers or a tongue tickling almost" (8). This negative depiction of the African woman reflects Wideman's own self-hatred, for one cannot hate that which is like his without hating his own. It is a reflection of Wideman's own running away from self that characterizes him, and his protagonist Cecil, during his early writing career. That is, the reader can use Wideman's depiction of African women, and his portrayal of European women, as a gauge of his African-centeredness, or lack thereof. Wideman's early African women are grasping, small-minded creatures whose saving grace is their physical likeness to the European, if they are related to the protagonist, or their religion. For Esther, religion saves her: "She believed their life together had been preordained by an all powerful force, and since this source was God in heaven, the joining of their lives had to be right no matter how far this rightness might be submerged beneath the troubled surface of their days together" (9).

Although there are not many positive presentations of African women in the whole of his canon, Wideman's depiction of Esther in *Hurry Home* is easily the most negative characterization. Other female characters have at least one positive element, at least from Wideman's perspective: they are beautiful from a Eurocentric perspective; they are intelligent; or they are strong. Tanya in *The Lynchers* is strong and striking, perhaps striking in her strength for there is no indication that she is beautiful, despite her "features moulded from skin barely beige" (86). Another flat, African female, she is coldly removed from all around her; in fact, she rarely talks! She is the friend of Wilkerson, the intellectual protagonist of the novel, and theirs is a relationship involving little or no physical contact: "He remembered how she mocked couples clutching in public, her distaste for the sentimental formalities of courtship" (77). Not only do they not kiss, but also "they spoke rarely" (76). Wilkerson is left to guess at her feelings, her thoughts (77). And while Wilkerson is involved in the Plan, Tanya knows nothing of his involvement until the end of the novel, and then she coldly dismisses it as crazy: "It is insane. If there ever was such a plan, it was nonsense and anybody who'd see it otherwise is insane. Finish your coffee" (237). Overall, Wideman's early view of women may be summed up with the words Wilkerson uses to describe his mother: "His mother's body, female because someone had snatched something from the point of her groin and left a hairy emptiness, female because someone had taken two fistfuls of flesh and hurled them with such force against her chest that they had flattened and stuck" (149). It is a very sexist, arrogant conception of the origin of women. Even Littleman's African woman, Angela Rowena Taylor, is an exploitive bitch. Like a prostitute, when Littleman has money, she stays with him; when he is broke, she disappears (168).

The African women who appear in the Homewood trilogy are much more positively and substantially drawn because Wideman sees himself, his family, his race much more positively and substantially. He has moved closer to his center. Still, what lingers during this second stage in his writing career is his belief that African women who look like European women are more beautiful than those who don't. Thus, his consciousness of himself as an African has increased, but is not fully developed. But how can Wideman not think a European woman is the most beautiful since his family, the subject of the Homewood trilogy, possesses and admires those aspects most like the European—fair skin, long straight hair, thin lips. Even Bess, the main character of *Hiding Place* and one who has strength of will, is independent, and respected, takes pride in the long, straight hair that she and her sisters possess: "Nothing but good hair on your mama's side. All of us Hollingers had that long straight hair. Was a time I could sit on mine. And Freeda too when she married John French had that good hair all the way down her back" (129). Hair the opposite of Bess' is "nappy and dirt brown" (77). Food tastes good; people are good if they treat you right; hair is not good or bad; it is straight or curly, or somewhere in between. Beauty then is measured from without, from a Eurocentric perspective in Wideman's early works.

However, Bess, unlike Tanya or Esther, is a thinking, caring woman. She has an identity, and she develops throughout the novel. Perhaps most important she is one of the novel's protagonists: the first woman protagonist and the only woman protagonist in all of Wideman's novels. When *Hiding Place* opens, Bess is hiding out on Bruston Hill. Overwhelmed by the deaths of so many loved ones, including her husband and her son, she thinks physical isolation can protect her emotionally. Tommy, the other protagonist in the novel, teaches her that physical and emotional isolation is the same as being dead. Ultimately, she has to decide to die or to live. She chooses the latter. What Bess learns by the end of the novel is that living means involving herself physically and emotionally in the lives of others. By coming down off Bruston Hill to tell Tommy's story to the police, she takes the first step toward saving her own life. Since Bess is able to learn to confront reality, not run away from it, what is foreshadowed are later Wideman women characters who will learn to see beauty in themselves, their brown skin, full lips, cottony hair, big thighs and hips.

In *Damballah,* a collection of short stories on Wideman's family and the Homewood community, there are conflicting images of women, if the treatment of the color white can be used as a reflection of Wideman's view of the female's physical beauty. It is an ambivalence that shows Wideman's growing, but not fully developed consciousness of himself as an African. The more he becomes African centered, the more he sees beauty in "blackness". With the depiction of family members, however, Wideman still uses his early conceptualization of beauty, mainly because it is difficult to criticize those who have given you life, those with whom you are subjectively involved: "That's your grandmother, Hazel. Looks like a white lady, don't she? She could sit on her hair. Black and straight as any white woman's" (69).

Yet Wideman's movement toward African centeredness does empower him to look beyond his mother's and grandmother's "beauty" to see the sterile lives they lead, wives who have centered themselves around husbands and have de-centered themselves from the African community: "Because her body's outline not deepened by his weight is only a pale shadow, a presence no more substantial than what might be left by a chill wind passing over the sheet" (86). It is the men who give life to these women.

The color white is dominant in the collection of stories in *Damballah* and, as such, can be used to assess Wideman's consciousness in regard to women, in so much that essential to his depiction of women is their skin color. There are stories such as "Daddy Garbage" that aid us in understanding Wideman's view of women from the color perspective. In it is a description of the color white as that which "softened the edges of things, smoothed out the spaces between near and far" (31). In "The Chinaman," Wideman describes his own relationship with Judy, his European wife: "All hell breaking loose outside, but we were inside, cocooned, safe, together. I liked the isolation, the sudden detour" (90). Added together, both passages offer a telling appraisal of Wideman's relationship with Judy. With her, he could block out blackness and all that it connotes according to Western etymology: confusion, chaos, ugliness, sin, ignorance. With her, he could isolate himself in whiteness, a safe haven, since "whiteness softened the edges of things."

But while there are these old, leftover connotations of beauty and whiteness, there are new ones as well. In "The Songs of Reba Love Jackson," a story that is very much centered within the African community, the color white is depicted as negative; it is what exploits and oppresses the African:

> White hands were peeling away his skin. White eyes lay on him like a blanket of snow. White feet stomped on his chest. . . . He was too cold to be dead. He was some place where white people were talking and laughing. (127)

Whiteness is death, "the dying into a thousand pieces are white" (127). It is the black songs, i.e., the spirituals, of Reba Love Jackson that offer some semblance of comfort to those Africans saddened by the oppressive circumstances of life:

> And she put her hand over the phone and ask me tell everybody be quiet please. And after some shushing and having to go around and bodily shut some people up, Reba Love's apartment quiet as church on Monday. She still have her hand over the mouthpiece and say, "This is my old friend Brother Harris from Cleveland and he just lost his mama and he needs for me to sing." (112)

In this story at least Blackness, not whiteness, "softened the edges of things, smoothed out the spaces between near and far." It is a positive notion of blackness that Wideman moves closer to, a notion that he begins to link with the physical characteristics of the African woman. Reba Love is one example of this link. Kwansa, in *Reuben,* is another.

After reading a story like "The Songs of Reba Love Jackson," the image of the woman in *Sent for You Yesterday* appears as an anomaly, a regression, or better still, a digression in Wideman's depiction of African women.[2] Reba Love is the first fully drawn African woman who neither is a relative of Wideman's nor has some distinct European features. Her hair, "plaited over with cornrows no thicker than scars" (115), is not praised as being black, straight, and long enough to sit on. She is poor, the daughter of a single mother who daily scrubs the kitchens of white folks, then walks "five blocks and start cooking and cleaning all over again" for herself and Reba (128). A member of The Sanctified Kingdom of Christ's Holiness Temple, the kind of church that Wideman ridicules in *A Glance Away,* Reba Love has a love for her people that is celebrated in the spiritual and dedicated to African people: "They hear their stories in my songs" (123). Standing within Africanness, not without, Reba uses her songs to tell the stories of oppression and injustice that her people experience, believing that "We's All God creatures and it ain't in the Bible to sit in the back of no buses or bow down to any man what ain't nothing but breath and britches" (122). People like Reba Love Jackson are the heroines of Homewood because they are a part of the people, care for the people, share with the people. Someone who sings for Homewood. She is beautiful with, not despite, her hair "plaited over with cornrows no thicker than scars."

Perhaps it is the subject matter, Wideman's own family history, that makes *Sent for You Yesterday* a throwback in its depiction of women, for just as in *Damballah,* Wideman's stories concerning his female relatives contain the author's early conceptualization of beauty. This third work in the Homewood trilogy is all about family and, thus, the images of the women are superficially based on physical characteristics for the most part, and the characteristics are those of the European female. In referring to his grandmother Freeda, for example, Wideman writes: "She was a pretty lady. She had skin white as a white woman's and long soft hair she wore piled on top of her head. He loved to see her let her hair down and loved to watch her comb it because she hummed as she combed it down past her shoulders" (27). Seemingly, beauty is synonymous with white skin and long hair.

One of the main dilemmas of the novel is the death of Albert Wilkes, a death not resulting from a struggle to assuage the plight of Africans in Homewood who have to wait on the corner outside the Blood Bucket to let the Europeans pick and choose between them for a day's work; a death not resulting from the struggle to survive and, at the same time, retain some sense of manhood, even if it means robbing the white leeches of the community like Tommy does in *Hiding Place*; a death not resulting from an overdose of dope in an attempt to escape the harsh reality of what it means to be African in Pittsburgh in the 1930s and

40s. Rather, it is a death that results from Albert Wilkes's love of a married European woman, a love that does not result from a recognition of commonalities, same people, same history, same struggle; but a love based on skin color and hair length:

> And his fine woman whiter than his daddy's whitest dreams. So white she could be black if she wanted to. . . . Red hair splashes down to her shoulders. Her skin is like snow, like ice in the hard light, her wet hair black against its paleness. Perfect and naked as a statue he thinks as she poses at him. (72)

Perhaps, in another sense, Albert Wilkes's death *is* the result of dope. Perhaps it is an escape from the harsh reality of what it means to be an African in the United States of America in Pittsburgh in the 1930s and 40s because in bed with her he can gratefully forget that he is black and poor and one-third less than a man. With her, "they played under satin sheets. Black so he couldn't see her and she couldn't see him so they had to find each other with toes and tongues and fingers and breath" (72). It is the kind of escape that Wideman himself indulges in and criticizes himself for in *Philadelphia Fire*. It is the kind of escape that the men in Wideman's family seem to opt for, on one level or another. John French's admonishment to Albert Wilkes to "get your nose out that white woman's behind" (66) rings hollow in light of the fact that his own nose is in a white-like woman's behind: "His woman [Freeda] moving naturally and unaware in nothing but her ivory skin" (82).

Even the one "black" African woman depicted in *Sent for You* who is characterized as beautiful has long black hair and is described as "ivory snow black." Samantha is "a good-looking woman too. Long dark hair and coal black. Kind of girl with that velvety smooth skin. When I hear beautiful African queens, Samantha comes to mind. She's the image. Black and comely. You know what I mean. Ninety-nine and forty-four one hundredths percent black. Yes indeed. Ivory snow black" (123).

There is one African female who has some kind of character outside of skin-color and hair: Lucy Tate, the Alice of *A Glance Away*. What characterizes her is not so much how she looks as how she is: "Lucy Tate trudging up the hill like she's bearing her cross and toting one for everybody else in Homewood on her scarecrow shoulders" (128). It is she who assumes the role of head of household for the Tate family and mother of Brother, despite her younger age. It is she who is credited with getting Doot (i.e., Wideman) on his feet to dance, to go for himself, to strike his own path/way in the world. But for all of these positive characteristics, she still seems only partly drawn. The reader rarely gets her side of the story. More a fleeting image of an independent woman with a sense of self-security, her character is only slightly more drawn than the Alice of *A Glance.*

Once Wideman is outside of the confines of family, he picks up where he left off in "The Songs of Reba Love Jackson" in his depiction of African women. Like Reba Love, Kwansa in *Reuben* has an identity of her own that is not dependent on long hair and white skin.[3] A prostitute, poor, dark, and a single mother, Kwansa struggles to raise her son without the support of husband, mother, father, or cousin. It is the kidnapping of her son by his father and the struggle she and Reuben wage to reclaim him that is the plot of *Reuben.* Toodles, a lesbian, also has character. She "knew who she was, what she was, and wasn't shamed of none of it" (47). These two women are the first of their kind. Omitted in earlier works, they are celebrated here as women who struggle within the African community to eke out a living for themselves. Overall, *Reuben* is a tribute to the common, everyday, struggling African woman. Both Toodles and Kwansa are respected by Wideman and the reader because of their courage and strength to overcome the obstacles of daily life in the ghetto. *Reuben* too is a tribute to Wideman, for in choosing to tell the story of community women, not men, he reveals his own growing consciousness about the struggle of women. And in characterizing these women as positive forces, Wideman had to have juxtaposed his own family with these Africans and found that its struggle to survive pales in comparison.[4]

There are several indices of Wideman's questioning of long-held assumptions of women. First, he questions the notion of "if you're white, you're right": the idea that skin color brings with it those rights that every and any human being should be assured of. When Kwansa struggles by herself to get help to find her son, she thinks of the basic inequality of the society in regard to women like her, that help would come and come fast if you were white or white-like:

When you were prettier, smarter, they had to treat you better to get what they wanted. Take a little time with you. Give you little things. There'd be a song maybe they sing at you. A favorite place they'd take you to sneak away from everybody else. If you had that special look, the bright skin, the good hair they liked, you could have things your own way sometimes. (57)

Wideman's criticism of U.S. society does not stop short with those who have some power and authority, but it extends to those Africans like him who "fall for the injustices," who go along with the piper by thinking that their "bright" skin and "good" hair make them better than other Africans. These petty bourgeois Homewood Africans Kwansa had known all her life:

Their names are like flashes of light, gone as quick as they come, never lifting the darkness yet tickling it, teasing a corner of her eye, gone before she can speak to them. They are gathering round to listen to her story, and when she has nothing to tell them they'll start talking nasty about her. (58–59)

Not only are these light-skinned Africans not better than Kwansa, but they're worse because their view of themselves as superior perpetuates the myth of the dark-skinned African as inferior and thus ugly. It puts them in league with the very system that is oppressing them. Their talking "nasty" about a fellow African who is darker-skinned and in trouble reveals their own lack of consciousness.

Perhaps Wideman's greatest tribute to African women is his historic appraisal of their continual sacrifices and contributions to the survival of the race, a tribute that does not set up class distinctions between African women who have light skin or dark, short hair or long:

Whose singing do you hear now? Shuffling chains dragged like a chorus of mourning women by the hair by the feet you trample them to make them sing. Divas, sweet mamas, Malindy, the fallen empress and lost ladies, where are they now? At your feet now, under your feet. African queens the spoils of war, the long train obscured by wailing dust, dust clouds and dust roosters and plumes of dust swirling like a feathered headdress over these captives dragged from the Land of Spirits. Say hi to your mama, your sister, your daughter. (203)

Certainly, *Reuben* marks a qualitative development in Wideman's canon. In depicting the struggle of the everyday African woman, he places himself in the center of Africanness. In paying tribute to her, he pays tribute to himself.

Wideman's appreciation of African women, revealed in *Reuben*, frees him to examine his own relationship with women, his attraction to European women in general, his wife Judy in particular. Interestingly, the inscription to his next novel, *Philadelphia Fire*, is "To Judy—who teaches me more about love each day." A complimentary one, the inscription is one the reader cannot help but to question since, in this novel, Wideman offers his most personal, yet objective analysis of his relationship with Judy. The relationship—at least Wideman's appraisal of it here and in earlier works, based on superficial qualities of physical appearance, based on beauty standards set by the capitalist enslavers like Prospero, and based on Wideman's early Euro-centeredness, self-hatred, and need to escape—is not a complimentary one:

> In the stillness of our bedroom her breasts registers deep silence. She sighs, extension of the breast, the breast under which she hides in a cage of ribs her heart. One of my ribs, so they say. Never thought to ask which one. To claim it. . . . Rib bones delicate as rib bones when I trace them with my fingertip and she is fragile as the straw where you might stash eggs for safekeeping. . . . Her dark hair used to be long enough to cover her breasts. Now it only reaches the first swell where the flesh softens and understands exactly what it's supposed to do next. . . . I pull her silver-threaded hair forward so it drapes the first soft swelling. (104)

This description of Judy is one that is extremely disturbing for several reasons. First, Wideman stresses physical characteristics, not intelligence or character. Second, the emphasis on the frailty of the European woman is false and one that has been promoted since U.S. slavery and the rise of capitalism.[5] Third, smacking of male chauvinism, he seems to derive comfort from the notion that women, including Judy, received life and substance as a result of him: "One of my ribs, so they say."

The passage refers to the time when Wideman is in Laramie, Wyoming, in his private world, isolated from any African connections, whether family or community or point of view. This view of the European woman is not unlike that of the European woman

Albert Wilkes is involved with in *Sent for You Yesterday*. It is a per-spective that reflects the extent of the African male's estrange-ment from self. Either a self-abdication, self-hatred, or a need to possess what the "master" owns, Wideman's interest in small, shapely, seemingly fragile European women—an interest which appears throughout his canon— reflects the author's orientation toward Euro-centeredness and his acceptance of the capitalist cre-ated myth of the "white" woman on a pedestal.

That the European woman is fragile, in need of protection by the male, including the African male, while the African woman— the Kwansas and the Toodles—are tough enough not to need a man at all is a conceptualization of women that has its roots in slavery. This picture is an ambivalent one, however. While the standards of beauty are reserved for those women of European descent (beauty standards are learned; no one is born with them), these women lack strength, character, and intelligence. They are the media-created, billboard images of European women; they are like the woman Cudjoe peeps at out his window: "The woman in the window possessed no insides. No periods. No illnesses, no female disorders. Wouldn't age or die" (56). A cardboard Euro-pean woman.

But when you marry based on these myths, you're bound to be disappointed. Sometimes, the under-the-cover, childish games of escape are not enough for the adult:

> This time, this age when we huddle under the covers and imitate ourselves as children playing in other rooms, other cities [other worlds]. All over again. Safe the way our children were safe. Leftovers and remnants and day-old goods tasting stolen and better than ever some nights. Other nights the edginess, the anger, the sense of loss, the fear, so I flip-flop, ply the channels like a ghost, waiting for some-thing to watch. (103)

There is a sense of loss, regret that colors this passage. Conditions which make Wideman and Judy huddle under the covers in a private world untouched by racism and the overall hardships of an interracial marriage have to negatively impact upon the rela-tionship, despite the reward of feeling as though he has enjoyed the fruits of something stolen (the master's wife?), especially for a thinking intellectual like Wideman who is growing more African-centered with each novel he writes.

In fact, *Philadephia Fire* reveals that Wideman understands something of the myth that he has bought into. In the Prospero-Caliban section of the novel, he explains how Prospero— the imperialist, the Great White Father—uses his own daughter Miranda to help enslave Caliban, to subjugate him and to steal his land:

> She's [Miranda's] trying her best to be her own person. She wants to share. But she can't. She's a prisoner, too. Hostage of what her father has taught her. A language which Xeroxes image after image of her father, his goodness, his rightness, his deed to the island and the sea-lanes and blue sky and even more than that. The future. Which is also confirmed and claimed in the words he taught her and she taught Caliban, buried of course, unmentionable of course, like her private parts, but nonetheless signified in the small-print forever-after clause of the deed. Her father needs her to corner the future, her loins the highway, the bridge, sweet chariot to carry his claim home. (141)

In many ways, it is a subtle, vicious process— colonialism (capitalism)—for in its use of "white" language and "white" women it lays a trap for the African male. And in doing so prostitutes the European woman, makes her slave too. That Wideman is aware of this reality, yet immersed in it reflects the crisis of the African Personality that many African males confront.

Some Africans, however, have always resisted the Mirandas, have known of the trap, or if not, have cared more about their own environment, their "black-eyed Susans," so as not to be lured by the trap, indeed not to even see that there was a trap. Unfortunately, Wideman was not one of these. He was snared. Yet, his open admission of his entrapment reveals his struggle to reclaim his African Personality.

4

"The Mis-Education of the Negro": The Intellectual and the Community

One of the most striking evidences of the failure of higher education among Negroes is their estrangement from the masses, the very people upon whom they must eventually count for carrying out a program of progress.

—Carter G. Woodson[1]

Just as Wideman's treatment of women can be used as a gauge of the author's growing consciousness of himself as an African, so can his treatment of the intellectual. With each succeeding work, Wideman increasingly understands the role the intellectual can and should play in relationship to the African community so that by *Reuben* and *Philadelphia Fire* the intellectual is one who acquires knowledge and uses it to help his people. However, in the first phase of Wideman's writing career, the intellectual is completely estranged from the community, thinking that involvement with his or her people means losing one's knowledge. Instead of viewing the African community as a place in which to share, apply, and test one's knowledge, the European-centered intellectual is one whom Carter G. Woodson refers to in *The Mis-Education of the Negro*. In the second phase, Wideman places himself in his writings for the purpose of self-appraisal. Looking at himself objectively as a character, Wideman is able to learn from his findings and to use his discoveries to aid in his self-development. The third phase marks Wideman's heightened consciousness of himself as an African in that he depicts himself as the intellectual who plays a contributing role in the African community.

The intellectual in *A Glance Away* is represented by both the African female, Alice, and the European male, Thurley. Alice, like

Wideman, wins a scholarship, goes away to college, and returns, feeling completely isolated from the African community. In conversations with the protagonist, Eddie, she tries to explain her feelings of isolation:

> Why I see you and no one else in the neighborhood. It's not that I think I'm better, it's just that I have absolutely nothing to say to them. I feel like a fish out of water. But I know this is my water, my home, that I can't ever change. And I want so much to have someone to share what I've learned, to have it flourish here. A person to help me keep alive the little something different I've felt grow up in me. Someone to preserve it, to protect it. I don't want to fall back, back into this. (116)

For Alice (and the early Wideman), mingling with the community means falling back into blackness, a primitive, ignorant, chaotic environment filled with all sorts of unsolvable problems. It is a blackness that is contagious; if the intellectual interacts with the community, s/he too will be infected by the chaos and ignorance of the masses.

With Thurley, there is not even the consideration of mingling, except for deviant sexual reasons. Otherwise, Thurley stays in his own world of aloofness, alcoholism, and aborted sentences:

> I loved the little nigger [a twelve-year old African boy Thurley picks up and molests], Thurley thought drinking alone. If love comes into this cluttered world, it is in the quiet space between orgasm and not orgasm.
>
> The thick blue book was opened. It was a diary, album, commonplace, letter, scrap, miscellany optimistically inscribed on its opening leaf *These fragments I have shored.* Thurley wrote: April 21, Easter Eve: Consummation—the momentary reconciliation of black and white in the heat of coition. I have paid for it with her [ex-wife's] jewel of great price. (40)

Even in Wideman's first work then, there is a dilemma confronting the intellectual. On the one hand, he can neither wholesomely immerse her/himself in or extract her/himself from the community, problem-free. Immersion means involvement which may "black out" the intellectualism of the intellectual. On the other hand, isolation means loneliness at best, behavioral deviance at worst. Thurley, Alice, and Eddie are characters who "leave" in some way, either physically or mentally. Each is isolated from family, friends, and community. When each ventures out to mingle, s/he is burnt in some way and comes running back to his/her respective holes. For instance, Thurley's weekday excursions to the classroom are catastrophic for him, so much so that he must steathily take a drink from the flask hidden in his office desk drawer. But even the drink is not enough to give him the courage needed to "connect" with his students:

> They [the students] wait for me to play the fool, to live up to the stories that circulate about me. A clown, a showman, who, if they're patient, they may see pull some colossal blunder, involve himself in one of his periodic scandals which they can say they saw enacted live onstage. Thurley teetered, dangerously close to falling from the edge of the desk. He experienced the profound vertigo of absolute solitude in a crowd. The eyes of his students were glazed over, and they saw nothing. Their lips were sealed, they spoke nothing. Their ears were clamped shut, and they heard nothing. (35)

Alice rarely comes out of her hole. On one of the few occasions in which she does—to connect with Eddie, she remembers not the positive they've shared, but the negative. Eddie's one fatal mistake is sleeping with Alice's European girlfriend: "And all I gave you were willing to trade with that whore for a smell of her white ass. Something rose in Alice and burst" (119). The memory sends her reeling back in her hole. Eddie's attempt to connect with his mother and sister are just as disastrous. When he does venture back to the source, he commits an even more foul act than that of drug abuse and neglect. He murders his mother (129–30).

Cecil, the intellectual protagonist of *Hurry Home*, harbors romantic notions of the African masses, just as a European would, seeing the laborious, penny-ante work of a shoeshine boy as that which should be accompanied by the playing of "some musical instrument—a guitar, a fiddle. I would play beside the boy, accompanying him along the street" (32). It is a naive view which holds the seeds of its own destruction, for Cecil who approaches the street-wise youngster from this perspective quickly gets burnt. He is tricked into getting a shoeshine, thinking it's free and then when he walks away without paying is hounded by the community men. The shoeshine's view of Cecil, on the other hand, is quite accurate: "Never seen a fool like that. Like I'm out here for my health. Free. Did that nigger say I said free shine" (32). This experience shows the reader, though not Cecil, how far removed the protagonist is from his identity. Trained as a magistrate (his term, not mine), the only African admitted in his class, he neither sees himself nor his community realistically. Being isolated, the African intellectual is a victim, a pawn just as any European entering the community would be.

Just to what extent the African intellectual is isolated is depicted by Cecil's tendency to wallow in self-pity, not unlike Thurley of *A Glance*. For example, instead of trying for another child or adopting one, Cecil grieves for his miscarried son, Simon: "I am willing to go on. I will breathe, shave, fuck. I will be a man of all seasons. But I will not undam those squiggles of other Cecils" (152–53).

So estranged is Cecil from his wife, family, and community that he is like a mind extracted from the body. His life is all thoughts and dreams. There is even the strong suggestion that Cecil's adventures throughout the novel—in fact, the novel itself—are all a product of Cecil's imagination. The last two lines of the novel read: "Cecil in the chair, Esther sprawled naked on her naked bed. Moonlight, starlight, the silvered dreams trembling imperceptibly as mute, indifferent spirals twist through them externally. So Cecil dreamed" (185). Seemingly, this dream-life is the result of Cecil's inability to find his niche in life, his rejection by the European community, and his refusal to reintegrate himself into the African community. In fact, Cecil would rather see himself as one of a kind because "being one of *them* is as impossible, frankly, as is being one of us" (153). Cecil has the identity of "the exception" thrust on him by the European world, and he accepts it, allowing it to define him: "Choice two, choice two is unavoidable. Everyone likes to be thought of as unique, don't they. One of a kind, treated accordingly" (153–54).[2]

And what does it mean for Wideman to have concocted a story for the reader to believe in and then reveal, only at the end, that it was really not a story at all? Certainly, one significance is that Wideman has manipulated the reader as the magician does his audience, an intellectual game of the highest order. Like masturbation, the novel leaves the reader unfulfilled, wishing for the real thing. In its offering the reader, especially the African reader, nothing substantial, *Hurry Home* marks Wideman's highest acceptance of the Euro-centered perspective: the capitalists' manipulation of their own people—all hype, no substance.

Intellectually, *The Lynchers* is Wideman's attempt to move from pure thought as represented in *Hurry Home*, to action. According to Coleman,

> The characters' attempt to be a part of the community shows that Wideman has moved toward a view that the black intellectual should definitely play a role in the black community; [yet] the intellectual's eventual alienation from the community and destruction in *Lynchers* show that Wideman sees no possible place for them, to a significant extent because of the poor, oppressed state of the community. Comparison of *Lynchers* with *Glance* and *Home* shows that Wideman's conception of the intellectual's identity and role has broadened, but his conclusion about his relationship to the community remains the same.[3]

The Lynchers does indeed reflect the intellectual's failed attempt to relate meaningfully to the community, but it is an attempt nevertheless. Wilkerson, the intellectual in the novel, wants to act, to commit himself to do some meaningful act for the community, but wastes too much time thinking instead of doing. He is plagued by the indecisiveness and ambivalence that often characterizes the intellectual, so that the reader knows early in the novel that Wilkerson cannot be depended on for the execution of the Plan. Thus, when Littleman is hospitalized, incapable of being the leader anymore and the job falls on Wilkerson's shoulders, the reader already knows that the Plan, if it ever had any hopes of being carried out, will be aborted now. There are several passages that help support the notion of Wilkerson as all theory, no practice.

Early in the novel there appears a specific passage on Favrila Ivolgin, a character in a Russian novel who seems the mirror image of Wilkerson: "As soon as the moment for action came, he always seemed to be too honest to do anything that was too mean. (He was, however, always ready to agree to any petty meanness.) He looked with disgust and loathing on the poverty and downfall of his family" (68). Like Ivolgin, Wilkerson is forever prepared to think, but rarely acts. And like the Russian character, he (and the early Wideman) hold the victims of poverty responsible for their own victimization. The height of mental masturbation, Wilkerson's relationship with Tanya is based more in his imagination than in fact; contact is made on a mental, not a physical plane: "They spoke rarely" (76) and "He remembered how she mocked couples clutching in public, her distaste for the sentimental formalities of courtship" (77). Even their one attempt to kiss seems ephemeral since their bodies never make contact: "The partially closed door was between them, a shield obscuring half her body when he kissed her" (238).

As teacher, Wilkerson is again more thinker than doer. His voice, the vehicle needed to consummate the act of communication, is muted in comparison to the voice of the next door teacher, Edward, who *says* what he thinks rather than *thinks* what he thinks: "The voice [Edward's voice] continued but was lost in a cavern at the pit of Wilkerson's belly, a cave where his own voice often settled, curling in the void, swallowed but indigestible, a reeling fog that by inches could fill his whole being with gray sickness" (88). At the time when Wilkerson should be communicating with his own students, he's thinking of Edward's voice, the ability his colleague has for communicating and his own inadequacy to do the same.

In choosing a team he doesn't like because he's too ambivalent to know which one to root for, even Wilkerson's interest in basketball smacks of the indecisiveness of the intellectual:

> His favorite team, favorite because he could become more involved rooting against them than he could rooting for some other, had been knocked out of the playoffs. . . . It was best when he didn't know whether he wanted a shot to go in or miss, whether he hoped the referee would call charging or blocking. (90)

The joy Wilkerson receives from rooting against a team rather than for one is negative in that it reflects this indecisiveness, but it is also positive, in a sense, because at least it reflects his ability to know what's wrong, to know what to criticize, to blame, even though he does not know the solution. Perhaps it is this dialectic which causes his inaction. But the "Catch-22" is that before Wilkerson/Wideman can move to the point of discovering answers for problems—including those of family and community—he has to get involved. Littleman's appraisal of Wilkerson (i.e., Wideman's self-appraisal) is correct: "You're an ostrich with your yellow ass sticking up in the air but for the moment nobody's after it and maybe you can even believe your head will find something down there in the sand" (113).

Wilkerson's lack of knowledge of himself and family, symbolized by the nothing bits of information noted in his diary, also prevents him from moving from thought to action: "No mention of father, mother. Wilkerson was annoyed that the information tediously recorded yielded almost nothing about its author (74)." (Thurley too writes fragments, "bits of information," instead of complete sentences.) "The most startling characteristic of the writer was his uncanny ability to fit all he had to say within the space allotted by the calendar's framework" (74). Until Wilkerson discovers more about himself, including the extended self, he'll always be an outcast in the community, another Cecil at worst, Alice at best. A person who begins something when it is too late, or almost too late, as a way of ducking responsibility: "He had daydreamed and read longer than he should have so now a slight edge of urgency would have to propel him through his final preparations. Happens so often must do it on purpose, not allowing myself to get ready till it's just about too late" (91). Both Wilkerson and Wideman must learn that taking responsibility, and its ancillary—leaving oneself vulnerable, is a part of life; and self-discovery, the first step toward responsible action. The intellectual's quest for self-discovery is the focal point of the Homewood Trilogy.

In the Homewood Trilogy, beginning with *Hiding Place*, the intellectual is no longer hiding from himself. In fact, Wideman stops hiding behind fictionalized characters and, instead, puts himself directly into the novels—albeit in minor roles—in an effort at undisguised self-scrutiny. It is a looking and laughing at self through the eyes of others, since throughout the trilogy he is referred to in the third person. (It is not until *Philadelphia Fire* that Wideman uses the first person narrative for self-exploratory purposes). And seeing oneself through the eyes of others is an important first step in self-development: becoming a healed, whole person.

Quite appropriately, Wideman as character is first introduced to the reader as a disembodied voice. Bess refers to him: "His brother the one talk like he's part God and part lawyer" (45). Next, the reader sees him through the uncluttered eyes of Clement, eyes that are the mirror reflection of the community: "Tall man in a

suit ducked in the door and looked around real careful like maybe
he in the wrong place, like maybe he subject to turn around and
split somebody yell Boo real loud" (98). The fact that Wideman
unravels only bits and pieces of himself in this manner suggests
his vulnerability, his skepticism about finding out too much about
himself too soon. It is as if this first step, as novelist and character,
in discovering self—in venturing into the world of family and
community—is a baby step: tentative, shaky, fearful, but necessary.

Once the voice and the reflection are presented, the character
comes next. Wideman is revealed as one who has been away from
the community so long that he is out of touch with its dynamics;
literally and figuratively, he speaks another language: "*Budweiser,
please* is what he ordered. And Violet bringing him a beer and a
glass just as nice. He don't say Rock or Bud or Iron like somebody
got good sense. He have to go and say *Budweiser, please* like Violet
supposed to set something different on the bar nobody else ain't
drinking" (99). It is a language that not only sets him apart from,
but also sets him above, the community, at least from the community's (i.e., Clement's) point of view.

The reason for Wideman's being out of touch is the next piece
of the puzzle presented. He has distanced himself, mentally, emotionally, physically, from his family and from the African community. It is a distancing so complete that his Uncle Carl can't
remember where his nephew, the author, lives. All he knows is
that it is "out West with the rich white folks":

> How many times you told me Wyoming? Know damned well youall
> live in Wyoming. You been out there what . . . two, three years now.
> Moved out West when Tommy had his first trouble. Yeah. And I still
> go and say Colorado. You know what it is, babe? All them places sound
> alike. That's what it is. I think Wild West and white folks, and one
> place sound just as good as the other. (101)

Of course, one place is like the other in that neither has relevance
to Wideman's family or to the African community. And the connection between when Wideman leaves and when his brother's
troubles begin cannot help being made; neither can the conclu-
sion: that Wideman's leaving is his attempt to escape self, to run
from his brother (i.e., race), to isolate himself from his Africanness
and to surround himself with whiteness. It is an isolation which

of necessity gives him a distorted, opaque view of the community and its denizens, including his brother Tommy:

> Sometimes I get close to hating him. Everything inside me gets cold and I don't care what happens to him. I think about all he's done, all the people he's hurt. The way Mom is now. And that man who got killed in the robbery. I know it's not all Tommy's fault. I know he's a victim in a way too. But on the other hand he's hurt people and done wrong and can't expect to just walk away. But he does think he can walk away. Like he walked away from his wife and son. He's still like a child. He always wanted every day to be a party. It's that attitude I hate, not him. I want Tommy to live, to have a chance. I want him to be a thousand miles away too, but I want him to see what he's done. I want him to take responsibility. (102)

Ironically, the reader thinks of Wideman, not Tommy, when s/he reads the last line. Wideman's analysis of his brother's situation is one based on a Euro-centered perspective, a view that holds the victim principally responsible for his victimization. So the reader is very much conscious of the fact that although Wideman and Tommy are physically alike, "Clement felt the man's eyes. They were the eyes of the ghost [Tommy] on Bruston Hill" (104), they share nothing else in common, except perhaps their tendency to use running away as a solution to their problems. In fact, Wideman's running away, an escape that Wideman himself doesn't fully comprehend until *Philadelphia Fire*, seems more serious than Tommy's. Coleman agrees:

> In the overall context of the book, when John says that he comes close to hating Tommy at times, he certainly shows his lack of understanding. He is out of contact with the community and understands nothing about the toughness of the struggle that Tommy's generation has had to face. Tommy has slipped outside the main circulatory channels of the black tradition, but John is even further outside the flow.[4]

In striking contrast to Wideman is Carl, one who is completely in tuned with the community as shown through his ability to speak its language—you know, jive talk: "Go on, play it. You know that's my tune, Babe. Push it three or four times and bring your fine self back here and lay one of those Rocks on me" (103). However, despite Wideman's "sore thumb" position in the community—in

thought and deed, words and action—his return to it is commendable. One has to first walk in his brother's shoes and laugh at
oneself before being able to correctly appraise the Other. So while
Wideman is "a snooty, dicty-talking nigger" (149) in this novel, he
has shown his willingness to change. Otherwise, he would not be
holding himself up to ridicule this way.

  Damballah and *Sent for You Yesterday* continue Wideman's self-
revelations. More than criticizing his high-falutin ways, these
works reveal bits and pieces of Wideman's history with his family.
In fact, "the most important thing Wideman does in *Damballah*,"
according to Coleman, "is to describe the black intellectual-
writer's arduous movement back toward the black community and
black culture":

> Wideman understands from his reading of other black writers and
> from his interaction in the community that the intellectual-writer is
> not necessarily an outsider, as he is often depicted in the mainstream
> modernist tradition. He also now fully understands that black culture
> is rich and substantive and that the black intellectual can both benefit
> from it and play a role in developing it. But the black intellectual has
> a problem because he has alienated himself, and he must master the
> culture and work himself back into it.[5]

  In *Damballah* we learn of Wideman's love and practice of basketball ("His brother used to play there all day. Up and down all day
in the hot sun with the rest of the crazy ball players" [163–64]);
of his summer visits with his family once he's married to Judy
("His brother John came back here to play when he brought his
family through in the summer" [164]); of his failed relationship
with his father that drives him to substitute the white face of Clark
Gable for the brown face that is his daddy's ("The white man at
the mirror is my father" [134]); of his welcoming his fugitive
brother to his home in Wyoming and yet his reluctance still to
get involved with him, the rest of his family, or his community
("He has seen his brother cry once before. Doesn't want to see it
again. Too many faces in his brother's face. Starting with their
mother and going back and going sideways and all of Homewood
there if he looked long enough. Not just faces but streets and
stories and rooms and songs" [174]).[6]

  In *Sent for You Yesterday,* Wideman appears no longer reluctant
to connect, to not see the faces, streets and stories of his history.

Rather he appears more African-centered, embracing, not re-jecting, any part of his past. Beginning with his birth, Wideman eagerly retraces the family's roots: "I was born about six months before that evening in 1941. I was inside the weave of voices, a thought, an idea, a way things might be seen and be said" (93). We get the story of his relationship with John French, his first daddy, and the circumstances surrounding that relationship: " . . . I'm born. Carl's sister Lizabeth's first child. John French's first grandson. John French my first daddy because Lizabeth's husband away in the war. By the time Carl and my father returned from the Pacific, I was big enough to empty the spittoon which sat beside Daddy John French's chair" (116). How Wideman gets his nickname is another story which exemplifies his acceptance of and pride in his roots: "Soon after Carl returned home Brother Tate caught me by my arm and tucked me into his chest and named me *Doot*, one of the scat sounds Brother talked with in-stead of words" (116). All of these instances reflect the "new" intellectual who is Wideman, one who neither denies, nor reluc-tantly accepts, his heritage.

While the Homewood Trilogy primarily focuses on Wideman, the intellectual, and his relationship to his family, *Reuben* and *Philadelphia Fire* examine his relationship to the African commu-nity. In *Reuben*, the seemingly unlikely character, Wally (as well as Reuben), is the intellectual who is Wideman. It is through Wally that the reader learns the bits and pieces of Wideman's college days at the University of Pennsylvania, days in which he was pro-pelled toward Eurocentrism. At first, Wally kept to himself: "he trusted no one" (109). But soon he "learned to hate the face in the mirror. My own face. Hate it for giving in, hate it for not being the right one, hate it for hating itself" (112). The hatred made him run from his Africanness, escape by surrounding himself with as much that was European as he could embrace: language, writing style, spouse, environment. It is the running and the es-cape that is discussed most in *Reuben*: "If he [Wally] falls asleep his legs will run him awake again. Remind him they never stop running. He scared them one day into fleeing from blackness, from having nothing, and now they never stop, don't know how to stop" (29). Wideman ridicules this attempt to run away from all that had nurtured him by having his protagonist Reuben poke fun at Wyoming as the state which epitomizes the place which best

symbolizes the good ole U.S.A.—from the European's perspective,
that is:

> Reuben makes it a ranch. Home, home on the range. Blue Wyoming
> sky, gray waves of sage. Stars and Stripes crackle like tinsel in a fabu-
> lous sky. Everybody's happy, wherever they are, whatever they're do-
> ing. . . . daydreaming, nightdreaming, climbing a ladder of stars and
> bars to heaven and back. Yippee. I. Oh . . . (202)

It is a scene straight out of a cowboy movie where everybody's
happy, a scene populated by manly men—European men— like
Clark Gable, "brushing his teeth with Scotch, smiling in the mirror
because he knows he's doing something cute" (133). It is a scene
that those like the early Wideman may identify with in their
attempt to escape their African reality. In "Across the Wide
Missouri," a short story in *Damballah* that reveals Wideman's estranged relationship with his own father, Wideman admits that his
memory of a meeting with his father has become one of complete
fantasy: "there is a kind of unmasking. The white man at the
mirror is my father" (134). While Wideman's admission of this
fact is carthartic, the ridicule of it in *Reuben* reveals distancing,
objectivity, rejection. It—living the life of a typical European in
Wyoming—is such a ridiculous notion, given Wideman's African-
centered perspective, that it is funny. We—Reuben, Wideman, and
reader—can laugh together, now, because we share the same
perspective.

Reuben as intellectual is not free of illusions either, although
I'm not quite sure Wideman was aware of this fact when writing
the novel. Although Reuben's knowledge is used to help the community, it is a knowledge grounded in idealism. A mixture of
voodoo and charms are used to create the outcome Reuben
wishes. It is as if Wideman believes the intellectual has the power—
an abracadabra power—to create reality. It is puzzling then
that Coleman does not seem to see anything awry with this
perspective:

> As an intellectual-activist, Reuben is a mythmaker like Doot; in his
> fictions of his personal history that constitute part of his myth, Reuben
> develops the necessary values, approaches, and attitudes that will pre-
> pare him to take constructive actions in the black community. For
> Reuben, these fictions are empowering because they give him the

strength, direction, and focus to do his work. These fictions are set against the restricting, imprisoning fictions that the white society imposes from the outside on Reuben, on other black individuals, and on the black community. Reuben's fictions allow him to create illusions of progress, change, and movement over time in the black community and thus to help the community.[7]

Neither the fictions of European society nor those of Reuben are helpful to the African community. Rather than smash the myths and create truisms, Reuben resorts to magic which in the long run makes him less accessible to the community. Rather than relying on people power to support his efforts to create a more just environment for African people, Reuben relies on hocus pocus. It is significant then that Reuben's trailer, once mobile, becomes a fixture in the community: "To see Reuben now you got to go to him. Trailer sits in that vacant lot behind Hamilton over near the school" (6). Reuben's illusions set him apart from the community, immobilize him, de-activate him, mummify him.

The intellectual in *Philadelphia Fire*—having explored his estranged relationship with family and community (*A Glance, Hurry Home,* and *Lynchers*); examined and embraced his family roots (the Homewood Trilogy); and analyzed and ridiculed his reasons for self-hatred *(Reuben)*—is now prepared to assume an activist posture in the African community. Not only has Wideman seen too many lost sons (his mother's [Tommy], his own, and *MOVE*'s), but also he has seen himself lost. It is too much seeing to remain aloof. With such a heightened consciousness there seems only one of two choices for Wideman to make, die (stop writing) or get involved (write for your people). After realizing his own Prospero perspective in regard to the Calibans of the world, his son included, Wideman does in fact at first contemplate suicide:

A tug right and the car would crumple against a concrete embankment. . . . No urge to change the course of his history, however, was part of this moment. Rather, he sat in the driver's padded lumbar-supporting seat in awe. Astounded by the concatenation of accidents, of minute turnings, of one thing after another after another that had brought him to this moment. Choice, will, intent. How could he ever have imagined what the outcome would be that day, any day in his distant, distant past when he decided yes. (105–6)

It is the overwhelming distance between Wideman and the African community, Wideman and his brother Tommy, Wideman and his son—a distance largely created by Wideman's own fantasy living—that makes this suicide option seem realistic: "Say the word *father*. Now say *son*. Now think of the space between *father* and *son*" (103). For surely if Wideman had not attempted to escape his identity, he could have minimized some of the difficulties he confronts, foreseen that "a child lost cancels the natural order, the circle is broken" (119). Now, facing up to his lack of responsibility in attempting to thwart the sons' imprisonment results in overwhelming feelings of guilt that stop just short of suicide, but makes him "sad almost all the time and wonders if it shows in his face. . . . Half his face obliged to go on about the business of living, half as if asleep, dreaming over and over again the nightmare of his son's pain" (111). It is a sadness which comes from the intellectual's awareness of his part in the catastrophic present of African youth. As Timbo, the cultural attaché to Mayor Wilson Goode admits, "We did take over, didn't we. I mean, shit. We had the whole world in our hands and we blew it. Dropped it like a hot potato. Whew. I don't want it you can have it. Tossed it back to Daddy and exited for goddamn parts unknown. Kathmandu. Wyoming. You know what I mean" (182). And, of course, Wideman does know. It is a knowledge which makes him write *Philadelphia Fire* instead of committing suicide, the ultimate escape. In doing so, Wideman the intellectual begins the long, arduous task of accepting responsibility for what happened and what will happen to his people:

> She was permitting him to overhear what she told the machine. Polite, accomodating to a degree, she also maintained her distance. Five thousand miles of it, plus or minus an inch. The precise space between Cudjoe's island and West Philly. Somehow she knew he'd been away, exactly how long, exactly how far, and that distance bothered her, she held it against him, served it back to him in her cool reserve, seemed unable ever to forgive it.
>
> How did she know so much about him, not only her but all her sisters, how, after the briefest of conversations, did they know his history, that he'd married a white woman and fathered half-white kids? How did they know he'd failed his wife and failed those kids, that his betrayal was double, about blackness and about being a man?

... that he was someone, a half-black someone, a half-man who couldn't be depended upon? (9–10)

In his acceptance of his past mistakes, in his struggle to come up with answers that will prevent future fires that originate from Africans' own self-hatred, people like Goode and himself, Wideman redeems himself.

In many ways then, *Philadelphia Fire* is about Wideman's own internal fire, a fire that completely burns out the old European-centered perspective and gives birth to a new African-centered one. It is a baptism of fire that whips the intellectual Wideman home, that drives him to reclaim his African Personality, just as it drives Cudjoe home: Back Again, Black Again. Home.

5

Thinking Black, Writing Rap:
Wideman and the Writing Process

A third method of evaluating Wideman's increasing development toward an African-centered perspective is by assessing his theory of the writing process. Early discussions on the writing process emphasize the pleasure or difficulty of writing; that is, the perspective is purely subjective, concentrating on the writer's relationship to his work. In his transition from Eurocentrism, writing becomes important because it tells the truth to the people; the reader, not the writer, is the important factor in the equation. The emphasis in later works is on neither the writer nor the reader, but on the purpose or objective of the writing process. Thus, for the Wideman of *Reuben* and *Philadelphia Fire,* the objective is to move the reader from inactivity to activity; from passivity to protest; from theory to practice. Writing becomes important because of its potential to activate change, to spark the reader to go out and make the world a better place in which to live. All in all, the writing process is an additional gauge to measure Wideman's success in de-centering himself from the Western tradition and centering himself within his own cultural, literary tradition. Once he does so, not only does his writing purpose and his audience change, but also his narrative mode.

In the first period of his career, Wideman sums up his own development as a writer in the following manner:

> For me audience was something that I took for granted. My sense of audience came from my education up to that point, my sense of what the important works of Western literature were, my sense of the classics, my sense of the esthetics that govern those classics; and so I saw myself as writing for that tradition. The notion of a separate audience and the notion of another set of obligations that I might have as a

writer, was very faint indeed. . . . As I look back it seems to me that I was too easily seduced into believing there was only one way to do things and that my job as a writer was to learn how to do things that way and be accepted because I had learned to jump through the hoops in the proper way.[1]

As Wideman becomes more in tuned with family, community, and race, he admits that his purpose for, as well as his style of, writing changed radically. In a statement to Kay Bonetti concerning authenticating one's background as an African, Wideman states: "That's what I'm trying to get into my writing. The possibility of individual growth, coupled with the idea that a given culture can help you select or select for you a framework in which it's most natural to work and from which you draw your range of choice."[2]

That in *A Glance Away* Wideman chose to make his statement on the writing process through Thurley, a degenerate European, shows just how far removed the author was from reclaiming the African Personality, just how much Wideman believed that "to write the very best, didn't you have to . . . 'transcend blackness'."[3] Thurley's writings are read by no one but himself, despite all the hard work he puts forth. From his perspective and Wideman's, art is a beautiful, seemingly effortless natural gift that the artist presents to his audience, but in actuality the process is laborious:

> That's what makes the music of strangers so exquisite, what often makes it unbearable. It seems to come from nowhere, to be pure and unattainable. It seems to somehow make a link with what I've been clumsily seeking and by the perfection of this link seems to exhaust the source. But it isn't like that. It's dirty business, sweating, bitter work, like you've done, Al, like I must continue doing. (155)

But for all the difficulty in producing a piece of writing, Thurley lets it rot: "The books, the countless manuscripts yellowing somewhere, each the humble seercloth of some proud beginning. Why do you do it, why do you bother then?" (70). Writing for Thurley and Wideman seems devoid of value except for the pleasure they themselves derive from it. While they seem driven to continue for subjective reasons, there seems no role for the reader, unless it is to sympathize with or feel pity for the poor, hard-working artist. But for the reader to assume such a posture puts her in the position of hero-worshipper, a subservient position in which the reader looks up to the writer, not for his contribution to humanity, but for his status as writer. Based on this Eurocentric, capitalist notion of superiority and inferiority, the reader, far from sympathizing with the writer's pains (she herself may have experienced worse labor pains), is turned off by being put in such a position. Wideman humbles, and thus reclaims, himself later by admitting to Bonetti the absurdity of this view; given the chance, there are others with a clearer perspective who could write just as well as he: "There are a whole lot of winos and junkies who have been alienated from their society and stand on the outside—who have the perfect angle for writing novels—but they're killing themselves, not producing art."[4]

Cecil in *Hurry Home* is Thurley in black-face when it comes to the writing process. Like his prototype, Cecil is totally engrossed in what he gets from his writing, not what his readers acquire:

> Since the artist can only call the process of creation itself uniquely, truly his own in a manner that not even the finished, public manifestation of that process is his own, the most pure art and the one perhaps most satisfying would be the most ephemeral art, the art that was all process, all unfolding, all experience, the art which remove the necessity of an exportable, finished product. (160)

The passage shows Cecil's/Wideman's lack of concern for purposeful art, that art which aims to contribute to the enlightenment, pleasure, and improvement of humanity, that Arnoldian "Sweetness and Light" that the reader derives from a good piece of literature. Indeed, in his ability to derive satisfaction from what he alone does with himself, Cecil is reminiscent of Toni Morrison's *Sula* who attempts to reach "post-coital harmony" with herself. But while masturbation may be seen as pure sex, it is not the most satisfying sex. It is only when one is joined with another in harmony can complete satisfaction be experienced. Wideman, however, does not fully appreciate such a relationship at this early juncture in his writing career. Rather, once again he emphasizes the pleasure and difficulty of writing experienced by the creative artist:

> The possibilities were endless and the challenges a limitation not of the medium but of the imagination of the challenger: size of rings, speed of rings, expansion outward, perfection of rings' shape (a badly

thrown pebble splashed so that the circle's shape was pitted, distorted),
more than one pebble would be thrown at a time to achieve subtle
rhythms, interlocking patterns of ring with ring, shadow with shadow.
And a moment after the pebble had stuck, after the creator's eye
had been delighted or depressed the entire effort silently passes to
oblivion.

Fulfillment rarely and if it comes at all, unified too closely with the
process to be exhumed, made a monument. (*Hurry* 160–61)

Clearly, the emphasis is on the creator, in this case, the writer. But
there is evidence, even in the midst of this self-fulfillment achieved
by the artist, that Wideman does begin to appreciate the impo-
tence of art for art's sake, the importance of the other in realizing
a deeper, more complete satisfaction in both the process and
product, for the preceding passage results from Cecil's day-
dreaming while shampooing, processing, creating the hair of one
of the patrons of Constance Beauty Parlor. So while Cecil halluci-
nates about what he can do by and with himself, his feet (or rather
his hands, in this case) are planted firmly in the soil (i.e., hair) of
the African community. What more earthy, central place is there
in that community than the beauty parlor? That Wideman places
his protagonist here, rather than alone in his bedroom, when
Cecil daydreams of the creative process, suggests that he (the pro-
noun is collective, not vague) will come down to earth; that is,
become centered in African culture.

The Lynchers serves as a bridge between Wideman's first writing
stage and his second, not only in regard to the writing process,
but also as a gauge of Wideman's increased consciousness of his
African heritage. The two are inextricably connected. Littleman
is a more earthy writer than either Thurley or Cecil. He is a
character who is very much concerned with and involved in the
African community. And he writes too. Both are possible. Littleman's writing is sparked by his need to retain his sanity, to keep
his feet on the ground. That is, his writing reflects his attempt to
keep himself grounded in reality rather than his desire to escape
reality: "I used to write a lot. Writing cleaned me out. Cleared
the bullshit. . . . I know what's important to me and writing is an
extravagance I can't afford. But I still have to get the words out
or they'd spin around and spin around and give my mind no
peace" (112–13). While it is commendable that Littleman writes

as well as acts, that he writes for a purpose, it is unfortunate that neither he nor Wideman (at this stage of his career) understands that writing does not have to be a self-oriented act, an ineffectual luxury. Rather, writing has the potential to help bring about change in the community. In this work, however, violence is viewed as the only viable change agent.

Still, art is linked with purpose in *The Lynchers* whereas it is not in *A Glance Away* and *Hurry Home*. Until art serves some useful purpose—even if it is simply therapeutic, Wideman intimates, it cannot truly be free, imaginative, creative art: "I write at night. During the day I soak the pages in a basin. The water gains a bluish cast as the words dissolve. I dump the sodden unreadable remnants into a waste basket before I go to sleep each afternoon. The writing is a conscious attempt to retain my sanity" (*The Lynchers* 166–67). Eventually, however, purposeful art must move beyond serving the artist only or else risk the chance of being "sodden unreadable remnants." Purposeful art that is readable and lasting is that art which also serves the interests of others. That's the message conveyed in Wideman's second writing stage.

In *Hiding Place*, the first work in the Homewood Trilogy, the plain and simple message is "somebody has to go down there and tell the truth." This one line, which at first seems to pertain only to the theme of the novel, reflects Wideman's commitment to change his purpose for writing. Now, he'll struggle to make his writing meaningful to others. Instead of living up on a hill, engaging in flights of fantasy, the artist will come down to join the people and to struggle to help the people by revealing the truth. The last line of the novel makes this point quite clearly: "She's coming to tell them he ain't scared no more and they better listen and they better make sure it don't happen so easy ever again" (158). Wideman himself is no longer the Eddie who sees his salvation in the hands of an alcoholic European father-figure; he is no longer the Cecil who is too scared to mingle with his people, who is so isolated that he sees them as exotic and romantic, through rose-colored glasses; he is no longer the Littleman who only relies on writing to retain his sanity. Wideman is the artist who comes back to his people, who centers himself in the African community in order to help, and who, by doing so, heals himself: "Maybe I couldn't tell them the way the women in my family had told the stories, but maybe if I wrote them down. And this was part of literary [*sic*] but also it was a way of healing. It was a way of dealing with my own sense of loss."[5] And, in order to help, he must not only speak the truth, but speak the plain truth so that there's no chance for confusion. *Hiding Place* then utilizes a "plain talk" structure and language pattern. It is no longer just the getting there that's important, but the reason for getting there. In this respect, the work of art serves as an eye-opener for the reader (as well as the artist).

Damballah and *Sent for You Yesterday* stress the importance of the reader-listener relationship because now Wideman fully understands the necessity of helping the reader *see* the importance of the text. In "The Beginning of Homewood," Wideman is Reba Love Jackson who sings songs for the people to help them get over, under, within, between, on, and into the truth. In fact, the Homewood Trilogy is the song Wideman dedicates to Homewood just as Reba Love's "This Last Song's for Homewood." The reader is a witness in the story, a participant in the telling of the story in the way that African people responded to the call of the speaker in communal Africa, in the way that the congregation participates in the African baptist preacher's telling of his sermon:

> I was thinking the way Aunt May talks. I heard her laughter, her amens, and *can I get a witness*, her digressions within digressions, the webs she spins and brushes away with her hands. Her stories exist because of their parts and each part is a story worth telling, worth examining to find the stories it contains. What seems to ramble begins to cohere when the listener understands the process, understands that the voice seeks to recover everything, that the voice proclaims *nothing is lost*, that the listener is not passive but lives like everything else within the story. (198–99)

Yet, despite his positive growth toward an African-centered writing posture as evidenced in *Damballah*, Wideman still has some growing to do. For the major weakness in Wideman's theory of the role of the artist and the purpose of writing in this second stage is his belief that fiction is reality, that "telling the story right will make it real" ("Lizabeth: the Caterpillar Story," 60). Even the listener, in "The Beginning," lives within the story. Rather than the writer imitating reality, it is as if the writer, ie., the storyteller, creates reality, including the listener, by writing. In "The Chinaman," Wideman states: "If she didn't tell the story right, there would be no baby, shuddering to life in her arms when she runs through the crashing door" (85). Of course, just the opposite is true. There would be no story, if there were no baby shuddering to life.

Wideman seems more cognizant of this opposite in *Sent for You*. In equating art with music, he demonstrates that far from creating reality the artist welds together the bits and pieces of reality into a complete whole:

> Albert Wilkes's song so familiar because everything she's ever heard is in it, all the songs and voices she's ever heard, but everything is new and fresh because his music joined things, blended them so you follow one note and then it splits and slimmers and spills the thousand things it took to make the note whole, the silences within the note, the voices and songs. (189)

The point is that the artist helps us make sense of reality by showing us the connections.[6] And in so doing, he helps the reader to see more clearly ("everything is new and fresh"), not see what was never there. The artist's, including the writer's, role is to push us to another level of understanding and awareness because he presents the connection between things that the reader may not otherwise see: "The sky colors are like bits of music. He [John French] can remember the oranges, the reds, the purples. They flash back to him, he can see them, but he can't put them together the way Albert puts together the chords, the phrases, the bits and pieces" (86). For Wideman, the artist, this quilting process does not merely involve those things in the present, but those in the recent past; past, past; past, past, past—circles of time are brought together to aid the reader in "seeing." Uncle Carl describes this idea of perception when he talks about Wideman the toddler and Wideman the adult: "Circles and circles and circles inside circles. . . . Point is I can see him back then just as plain as I see him now and it don't make no difference. Just a circle going round and round so you getting closer while you getting further away and further while you getting closer" (118). In art's ability to "carry you away," there's a fringe benefit that the artist offers the viewer/reader/listener as well—temporary escape, a safe haven from one's present, one's dimension, one's self: "Brother could draw. It was like listening to people who can really sing or play an instrument. Doesn't matter what they play or sing, they put you in it and carry you away" (194). It is a "second sight" made possible by Wideman's African-centered perspective, a view that allows him to see the relationship among things, events, people: That the African's exploitation and oppression is directly connected to the capitalist's prosperity. That the African intellectual is connected to the African community. Wideman writes:

> The novelist or the writer is a storyteller, and the process for me that is going to knit up the culture, knit up the fabric of the family, the collective family—all of us. . . . And so that storytelling activity is crucial to survival, individual survival, community survival. So the storyteller, the artist, is a crucial member of the community.[7]

In *Reuben* the emphasis is less on the reader and writer and more on the potential of the finished product to change the world, to make it a better place. In his attempt to emphasize art's more practical, more purposeful aspect rather than its aesthetic qualities, Wideman utilizes the law, not music, as an example of the power of writing:

> The law was a series of steps. Each step depends on the one before it, as he'd assured the young woman in his office. The law created its particular fiction of motion, its metaphysical passage from disorder to equilibrium, unfair to fair, chaos to order, by establishing a series of steps—a due process. If those steps are followed, so the fiction goes, there is motion, progress, results can be reached, the world made a better place for litigants, for all of us. (16)

This new emphasis on art as catalyst of change marks Wideman's return to the African community and its interests. Anyone who is African-centered will not only see the problems experienced by his people, but also will use his skill, whatever it is, to help solve these problems. Logically, Wideman's view of the writer had to change, for he himself changes. No longer the European-centered writer who focuses on self and, in so doing, sees himself as great and calls upon his readers to sympathize with his labors, Wideman is the Malcolm with a mission. Just as the lawyer Reuben can serve some practical purpose in solving the problems of a Kwansa, so Wideman the writer can serve some practical purpose in solving the problems of African people.

Not only does the writer have the opportunity to save someone, he also has the power to immortalize one because books don't die. Wideman's comments on the photographer Eadweard Muybridge help us to understand this dimension of the writing process: "When he puts you in his camera he does not steal your soul. He opens its window. He builds you a pyramid and spares you the ravages of time. Beetles, worms, gravediggers and grave robbers and all the rest leave you alone and forget. You are young forever. Saved forever. As long as someone remains to look" (*Reuben* 21). The writer is historian, not clairvoyant.

It is to Wideman's credit that at the same time he sees the writer as chronicler and change-agent, able to contribute to the betterment of humankind, he also sees him as weak and ineffectual. If all the writer has to offer the community are words—words that may never be read, how can he compare with the activist, lawyer or otherwise, who is visible to and accessible to the community?

> Part of the world that went about its business ignoring words because words didn't matter, didn't care. Wind, sunset and sunrise, roaches, fire—no matter what words claimed, no matter how hard they tried to fool themselves and take the world to hell with them, Reuben believed certain things would persist, would find new colors and mate in new combinations, push up through the rot and charred rock, bloom again, ache again as his stubborn hands ached snapping and popping and pinching each other to life each morning. Plans were fermenting deep in green sap even now as words faltered on their last legs . . . desperate to keep their power, to be seen as well as heard, seen as real by weak creatures like himself who pretended they were authors of the universe. (*Reuben* 60–61)

Once again, Wideman's sense of inadequacy is directly related to his African-centeredness, for if he were not concerned for the African masses, then he would not be concerned that his words may not be enough to solve their problems. It is those in the African community who are less likely to read, yet it is they whom the conscious writer wants to reach, whom, in fact, this type of writer can most help. For this sector of the population in particular, plans and action are needed, plans "fermenting deep in green sap."

If writing is weak in its potential to effect change, so is it potentially harming for the writer, for it can snatch him right out of reality, as it did Wideman. It can serve as a conduit straight to fantasy world:

> Had he somehow helped cause his brother's plight? Did years of neglect, careless stowage on the bottom layer of a bottom box, burial under sheaves of yellowing pads, did all that equal turning a lock, throwing away a key? He couldn't know for sure and that vexed him, but he knew he was responsible now, that the image of his brother he'd salvaged depended on him and he depended on it, whatever it was. (*Reuben* 67–68)

The artist cannot afford to escape because not only does he neglect his responsibility as his brother's keeper, but also (or as a consequence?) he neglects himself. For what happens to one's brother, happens to oneself.

Wideman's act of de-centering himself from the western tradition and centering himself within his own cultural tradition not only makes it possible for the author to understand what he should write about and for whom he should write it, but also how he should write it. If writing is important because it tells the truth to African people, than what more appropriate structural forms to utilize in this truth telling process than those that best imitate those of the audience Wideman is trying to reach? So just as purpose and audience become African-centered so does the literary form. To be truly effective, the artist must match form with content; enhance message by creating a structure that grabs and maintains the reader's attention. Beginning with *Reuben*, but most pronounced in *Philadelphia Fire*, Wideman creates innovative narrative forms and voices, grounded in the African tradition, as conduits for his messages.

In *Philadelphia Fire*, Wideman seeks the creative narrative structure of the jazz musician, a Charlie "Bird" Parker structure that not only pays homage to what has come before, but a structure that creates anew. Like Bird, the later Wideman is a mockingbird who takes off "on the songs of other birds [African writers], inflating, inverting and turning them wrong side"[8] (Ellison, 223). Henry Louis Gates, Jr. describes this kind of creativity as intertextuality, "a process of repetition and revision" or signifyin(g), "a metaphor for textual revision."[9] One of the narrative strategies that Wideman repeats and revises is that of the more than one-voiced narrative mode. In *The Signifying Monkey*, Gates describes the double-voiced narration.[10] Wideman revises this concept to create a triple-voiced narrative mode. In *Philadelphia Fire*, the narrator starts off as an omniscient narrator ("Cudjoe watches the sea cut up" [4]); becomes a character, Cudjoe, an instructor who teaches Shakespeare in a way that African children can digest him, an African-centered way ("I think back to the beginning. When the project was just an idea teasing me. Black kids doing Shakespeare. How impossible it seemed" [134]); and reincarnates into the author who, after his son's imprisonment, finds writing impossible:

> But it was so hard to write. I'd get an idea of how to describe the moment I was wounded and the period right afterward when my illness began. At last I'd turn up a good idea. So I began to hunt for words to describe it and finally I thought up two. But by the time I got to the third word, I was stuck. (107)

By quilting together these narrators in a single text, Wideman creates a triple-voiced narrative structure. But, even more important, he recaptures the collective voice, the collective worldview, of traditional Africa that was lost during the African's slave-making process.

Another strategy that Wideman employs is what Gates calls the "speakerly text," a text whose rhetorical strategy is designed to represent an oral literary tradition.[11] Of course, the "speakerly text" is not new in the African literary canon. Paul Laurence Dunbar, Zora Neale Hurston, Alice Walker, and others were/are masters at creating characters whose voices simulate those of some sector of the African population. Within the folk tradition as well, mimicking was an important tool used to outwit or poke fun at the slavemaster. Still earlier, the griot in the West African tradition can be seen as the master of voice simulation in his role as storyteller and historian. But the speakerly text is new to Wideman. In the Shakespeare section of *Philadelphia Fire*, Cudjoe uses the African vernacular to teach his students *The Tempest*:

> Mr. prosperous Prospero who wielded without thought of god or man the marry ole cat-o'-nine tails unmercifully whupping on your behind and still would be performing his convincing imitation of Simon Legree, of the beast this very moment, in this very classroom, cutting

up, cutting down, laying on the stripes, if it weren't for me, girls and boys. Your big boppa, name droppa, cool poppa, daddio of the radio. (131)

This "hip-hop" mode of expression is clearly absent in earlier works such as *A Glance Away* and *Hurry Home*. Moreover, rejecting the standards of European literary tradition, Wideman comments on his own narrative structure within his narrative structure! He interrupts the Cudjoe story, has Cudjoe halt his teaching of *The Tempest*, to comment on the nature of narrative structure:

So this narrative is a sport of time, what it's about is stopping time, catching time. Watch how the play works like an engine, a heart in the story's chest, churning, pumping, tying something to something else, that sign by which we know time's conspiring, expiring. (133)

It is a structure within a structure within a structure just as Caliban's story is a story within Cudjoe's story and Cudjoe's story is a story within Wideman's. Layers of narrative structure have to be peeled away to reveal the thematic relationship among parts of the whole: Wideman's story is like Cudjoe's, and Cudjoe's (and all the other Cudjoe's, exploited and oppressed people) is like Caliban's. Once again, Wideman's narrative prose simulates the cyclic epistemology of traditional Africa: Everyone and everything is interconnected.

And why not burst the seams of narrative format as well? Wideman seems to ask. For, like the modern revolutionary poets— Haki R. Madhubuti (don l. lee), Sonia Sanchez, and Mari Evans come to mind, the African-centered Wideman even utilizes the printed page to convey, more effectively, the message to the reader:

What's the point?
    Doing it. That's the point. Why not? (*Philadelphia Fire* 133)

Clearly, Wideman's newfound style of writing is predicated upon his newfound Africanness, his reclamation of the African Personality, since his theme of active involvement in struggling against oppression in the African community is reinforced by an Africanized narrative voice and structure.

There are two additional ways in which Wideman demonstrates

his escape from the imprisonment of European literary standards. The first and most revealing example is the author's sati-
rization of the English language, a language that he so ardently
imitated in his early works:

> The lingo is English landwich. Quack of the baddest, biggest
> Quacker. King's English. Pure as his tribe. We've heard it before, leak-
> ing from a circle of covered wagons, a laager squatting on the veld, a
> slave fort impacted on the edge of a continent, its shadow athwart the
> deep blue sea, a suburban subdivision covenanted to a lighted shade
> of pale. You've also heard it on TV, if nowhere else, boys and girls,
> the slang of getting and spending. (129)

The English language is a language that consumes, "landwich,"
that eats up the language of the slave (or ex-slave). It is a language
of the slavemaster, whose drive in life was profit, "the slang of
getting and spending." It is a language that is slang just as any
other group or nation has its slang. No better, no worse.

The second example is Wideman's insertion of a letter written
to himself. The letter, among other things, reinforces the fact
that Wideman and Cudjoe are both characters and narrators in
the novel:

> Dear Mr. Wideman. On the Move!
>   I am writing to you because I read an article in a magazine and it
> featured a story or a piece on you. . . (124)

If not before, then certainly from this point on, the reader feels
comfortable accepting Cudjoe's experiences, thoughts, and words
as those of Wideman. This feeling of comfort allows the reader
to see the Cudjoe of the last paragraph of the novel as Wideman:

> Cudjoe hears footsteps behind him. A mob howling his name.
> Screaming for blood. Words come to him, cool him, stop him in his
> tracks. He'd known them all his life. Never again. Never again. He
> turns to face whatever it is rumbling over the stones of Independence
> Square. (199)

Just as Cudjoe refuses to run away again, so Wideman promises
his readers that he will "never again" run away. Both face their
Africanness, including the responsibilities that one inherits as a

result. Both free themselves from Eurocenteredness ("Independence Square").

All in all, Wideman's newfound style of writing is predicated upon his newfound Africanness. It is a style that recognizes, for the African, the laws of the "white man" don't jive. The standard (i.e., European) rules for writing do not fit the African context. They must be torn down and burnt up. So like Albert Murray in *Stomping the Blues*, Wideman

> speaks down home southern idiom . . . , urban street talk, academese, the argot of musicians, formal preaching, teaching rhetoric of the blues people who *know there* because they've *been there*. Not only does the voice command numerous varieties of language, it also has the musical sense of timing necessary for quick changes, shifts and counterpoint. The narrator creates verbal equivalencies of the strategies he identifies with the blues tradition in Afro-American music: improvisation, call and response interaction with the audience, riffing, breaks, parody and stylized quotation of a variety of sources.

This Africanized style of writing, it must be remembered, depends upon "a body of information shared by the reader and writer."[12]

And it is to Wideman's credit that he does not care whether or not this shared body of information is understood by outsiders. (For the writer, the outsiders are the critics.) As one who has reclaimed his Personality, Wideman knows all too well what happens when one allows others to define one's self or one's goals. *Kujichagulia* (self-determination) is the principle by which Wideman now guides himself. Just to make this point clear, Wideman uses his text to reprimand European critics who blindly or intentionally read and shape the African's work of art into what they want it to be. In the first section below, Wideman uses this European critic's own voice to explain this reshaping process. In the second section, Wideman criticizes the critic for distorting the text:

> "The plays really abut Prospero's guts. Everyman. The inner drama. The war of light and darkness within our souls. The power of the artist to create, transform. Poet as savior."
> You're too fat, Charley. Too fat, too white and too old. This is a play featuring shining black kids. Point of the whole thing is for them to

master Shakespeare. To learn from putting on the play. To teach their teachers and families. Maybe teach this whole neanderthal city what kids are capable of. You're something else. Charley. Cudjoe shares his idea with you and what do you do, you try and eat it. (145)

Charley is that critic who makes powerful African creations into existential universalisms. Only an African-centered Wideman could make such an assessment. He has so distanced himself from the European perspective.

Perhaps the single passage in *Philadelphia Fire* that best sums up the extent of Wideman's growth from Euro-centeredness to African-centeredness in regard to the writing process is the one that tells us, straight out and straight up, that action speaks louder than words:

> Better to light one little candle than to sit on one's ass and write clever, irresponsible, fanciful accounts of what never happened, never will. Lend a hand. Sit down your bucket. A siren screams. We should stop in our tracks. Walls are tumbling, burning-hot walls on tender babies. And you sit here mourning cause your welfare check's late. (157)

Wideman sets down his pen, or rather picks up action along with his pen, in order to take a more activist posture in solving the problems of the African masses: "Writing is, after all, an enterprise of the imagination. If you look too hard for the way that it impacts our real world, then you either get phony answers or half-assed answers or maybe just confused."[13] This statement by Wideman is one which is at variance with his earlier one which sees the writer as one who makes the world real: "Telling the story right will make it real" ("Lizabeth: the Caterpillar Story," *Damballah*, p. 60). Moreover, he entreats the reader, not to join him in his text, not to escape reality by joining the writer in the harmonious fictitious creation of another world, but to put aside the text, to become a part of this world by joining him in doing something about the problems.

6

"How Would *They* Know?": Conclusion

Just as I had completed what I hoped to be the next to the last draft of this work, Wideman published his third collection of short stories, *the stories of john edgar wideman*. I read the *New York Times* review of the collection before I bought it. In fact, it was the review which determined for me the necessity to include the collection in this work. For the review emphasized the beauty of the older, Homewood stories, implied in fact that the works included in the Homewood Trilogy were more lyrical and thus more powerful works of art than the more recent ones included in the new collection:

> Many non-Homewood stories in this volume tackle the thorny subject of relations between the races. . . . these stories are fairly conventional tales that could have been written by any competent graduate of a fiction-writing class. They lack the assurance of the Homewood stories and their ease of language and liberty of form.[1]

I was doubtful. How can the works produced by Wideman in his early, European-centered period be more powerful than those written after he had reclaimed his African Personality? It would be like saying a blind person could see better when he was blind than when he regained his sight. Of course, the critic's view is not one that is African-centered. Otherwise it would be more likely that the criticism would have been just the opposite: "Though lyrical Wideman's early Homewood stories lack the potency and relevancy of the new stories included in his recent collection." Interestingly, the critic reveals that for him or her the appeal of the Homewood stories rests in part on their "Faulkneresque" quality.

Before attempting to classify these new stories as better or worse than Wideman's earlier ones, perhaps it would be useful to discuss comments such as "fairly conventional tales that could have been written by any competetent graduate of a fiction writing class" and "lack the assurance of the Homewood stories and their ease of language and liberty of form". Is the choice of subjects or the language of the graduate student being measured? According to Frantz Fanon, "To speak a language is to take on a world, a culture. The Antilles Negro who wants to be white will be the whiter as he gains mastery of the cultural tool that language is."[2] That Wideman's language (style, in this case) in these stories is not Faulkneresque is a credit to him since it signifies his rejection of the western literary standards he had earlier embraced. The language (the use of the English language, in this case) of the graduate student must reflect good grammar and writing skills or else s/he would not be labeled "competent." To call stories which have as their subject matter apartheid, teenage pregnancy, and infanticide "fairly conventional tales" seems inaccurate as well.

Though I admit that I do not know what is meant by "ease of language" since "ease" means freedom from pain and only animals experience pain, "liberty of form" suggests creative narrative form. Structurally, the stories in this collection are Wideman's most creative, beginning with the use of lower case letters for its title and for the author's name. In this work, more than in the earlier ones, Wideman enlists structure in service of theme. "I'm no higher, no bigger, than the people whom I represent," he announces.

Clearly, Wideman demonstrates an increased consciousness of himself as an African in this collection. In fact, these recent stories almost pick up where *Philadelphia Fire* leaves off. *Philadelphia Fire* demonstrated Wideman's growing concern for African people in general, not just those of his family. In that work, he began to ask himself the "cause" question concerning the race: What is the cause of the African's exploitation and oppression? His answer revolved around the Prosperos, those early European capitalists, or agents of capitalists, who went around "discovering," exploiting, and oppressing other people for profit. In these new stories Wideman continues to probe the cause question by first looking at what happened to himself; then by looking at those like Robby, those not so conditioned by "the system", who grew up in Homewood; and finally by looking at what's happening to African people worldwide.

In "Backseat" Wideman gives us a glimpse of his early lessons in how not to be an African. He is taken by his paternal grandmother to the home of the Europeans she maids for because they have heard about how smart he is. While eating breakfast with them, his grandmother maiding all the while, he is so scared, so afraid of doing a "Nigger" thing that he eats what he hates: soft scrambled eggs (35).[3] His adult perspective on his conditioning is all different now from what it was in early works, including those in the Homewood series. Unlike the man/boy in "Across the Wide Missouri," Wideman's view of his father and his father image, Clark Gable, is at odds. Now this "white man tall in the saddle calling all the shots" is likened to those capitalists who have exploited and oppressed Africans and other people of color. He is the "Great White Father," this "white man tall in the saddle" who thinks of the world as "his world" (29). Wideman also learns that his "opportunity" to leave Homewood does not mean that everyone has that same opportunity, no matter how qualified they are, or that Homewood will benefit from that opportunity. Being "the only one" of your kind not only robs you of your identity, but also does nothing for the rest of the African world: "I thought when I returned home one time it would be different. I didn't know exactly how but maybe better somehow" ("everybody knew bubba riff," 72). One of his old running buddies "schools him" that his leaving didn't change things for them or Homewood: "cause everybody knows the way it goes moving west mister moving on out bro up and out to star time don't fuck with the product" (73). The language, in slang and elliptical, reinforces the notion of just how broken up things are in Homewood. Far from making conditions better, opportunities for a few Africans have often served to rob the African communities of their most valuable resources. Those with the most potential to give and to share have been extracted from the communities just as the slave trade robbed Africa's best, those who were between the ages of five and thirty-five, and left the infirm and the elderly to survive as best they could.

The reader gets a better glimpse of Wideman's increased understanding of the cycle of oppression experienced by African people when he discusses the future of African males:

all the brothers got a chain round they necks and a number on the chain and somebody pulling numbers daily bang bang down you go

it's just a matter of time bloods be extinct you know like them endan-
gered species and shit don't laugh it's true we ought to fire up a
campaign shit they got one for elephants and whales and ring-tailed
sap-sucking woody woodpeckers why not posters and TV ads and
buttons and T-shirts *S.O.N. Save Our Niggers* (71)

The passage lacks punctuation; sentences are all run together
suggesting the chaos and decay of African communities and the
loss of African values and lives. Structurally, then, the passage
reinforces the idea of oppression in the African communities that
Wideman is attempting to convey.

Rodney King is an example of one of those "black boys" who
fights in U.S. wars, manages to stay alive, and then comes back to
potential or actual extinction. Who else is Wideman referring to
below as the "black man beat to his knees by a whole posse of
cracker cops"?

Then what will those black boys think who risked their lives and lost
their lives to keep a grin on the face of the man who rode Willie
Horton bareback to the White House. Twelve, fourteen cops on TV
beating that boy with sticks long as their legs. Our young men not
even home good from the war yet. What you think they're thinking
when they see a black man beat to his knees by a whole posse of
cracker cops. Somebody ought to tell them boys, ought to have told
me, it happens every time. After every war. Oh yeah. They tell us
march off and fight in some jungle or desert. Be heroes and save our
behinds. We'll be here rooting for you. But when you come back across
the pond, if you make it back, don't forget where you are. You ain't
no hero here. You know what you are here. And in case you don't
remember, here's a little reminder. A forget-me-knot upside your
nappy head. Bop bop a loo bop. Bop bam boom. Rolling around on
the pavement beat half to death just in time to welcome our boys
home. ("Backseat," 28–29)

Wideman is not just concerned about the African male, but also
African children, the most vulnerable sector of the world. His
most creative work to date, "newborn thrown in trash and dies"
is a fine example of just how much Wideman has reclaimed his
African Personality. The voice, we discover well into the story, is
that of the newborn of the title, an infant girl thrown forty-five
feet out of a window into a trash bin. Her material conditions in
life, her environment, are so horrendous that in just the time it

takes her to be born and her nineteen-year old mother to throw her away, she encrues the intelligence of an elder. Out of the mouth of babes, or so they say. It is this "they" who are to blame for the conditions in which she is born and dies: "They say you see your whole life pass in review the instant before you die. How would *they* know" (120). It is a questioning/probing voice (the baby girl's and Wideman's), the voice of a thinking person free of the chains that have conditioned the African's mind for so long. (The infant has not been living long enough to be brainwashed and Wideman's "brain" has just been freed.) This freedom allows the narrator to look at U.S. society without blinders on.[4]

Born in one of the housing projects that breeds disaster, the infant uses the dwelling to size up the nature of capitalism in the U.S. Each floor symbolizes a particular class in the society. Using her quick downward flight to analyze the nature of each of these classes, she understands quite clearly that "each floor exists and the life on it is real, whether we pause to notice or not" (125). Appropriately, the bottom floor, the foundation of the building, is the most corrupt floor and happens to be that which represents the president of the U.S.:

> El Presidente often performs on TV. We can watch him jog, fish, travel, lie, preen, mutilate the language. But these activities are not his job; his job is keeping things in the building as they are, squatting on the floor of power like a broken generator or broken furnace or broken heart, occupying the space where one that works should be. (126)

Perhaps what is most unique about these new stories is that for the first time we get stories about the condition of African people worldwide. Wideman does not restrict his pen to the boundaries of the U.S. Perhaps his increased awareness of the Prospero mentality, discussed in *Philadelphia Fire*, has enabled him to see that the nature of capitalism has not changed significantly. Instead of individual representatives of capitalist countries going out to conquer new worlds and peoples, the countries themselves are performing these tasks. One thing for sure, Wideman notices that African people worldwide are suffering from the same conditions. While in South Africa, the narrator of "what he saw" makes the connection between living conditions there and in Pittsburgh:

"Acres of shanties, shacks, lean-tos, tents, shelters so mean and bizarre they take me back to the vacant lots of Pittsburgh, the clubhouses my gang of ten-year-olds jerry-rigged from whatever materials we could scavenge and steal" (96–97). And what happens to the people, the uprooting process in South Africa and urban renewal in the U.S., is the same: "In Georgia, Mississippi, South Carolina uprooted even after we're dead. Blades dig up our ancestor's bones, crush them, scatter our cemeteries to clear the way for shopping malls, parking lots" (98).

Not only are connections made between African people within the story, but also among stories. For just after the South Africa story—one about police brutality—appears a story about police brutality in an African community within the U.S., "a voice foretold." The story concerns the aftermath of an incident in which New York policemen force their way in on an innocent couple and murder the man—all in a case of mistaken identity, no questions asked, no apologies given: "What makes it so bad they [the couple] ain't never done nothing to nobody. Happy living together up in that apartment. Make you feel good when you see them on the street. One day in the prime of life. Next day those dogs come and both them children gone" (117). Unlike the South African story, however, this one sends a message that something has to be done, something will be done: "Think of up and down and paths crossing and crossing roads and crossroads and traffic and what goes up must come down and heaven's gate and what goes 'round come 'round" (119).

The extent to which Wideman utilizes African women as main or significant characters as well as the quality of the remarks he makes about them in this collection are refreshingly progressive.[5] In "Backseat" he remembers an occasion when he had a sexual encounter in the back seat of his Uncle Mac's 1946 red Lincoln Continental. He "opened her fat thighs, jiggly as they wanted to be, but like a compass too, hinged, calibrated so you can keep track of how far they spreading" (23). Here the African woman is not ridiculed for her "bushy hair" as in *Hurry Home*; the depiction is more positive because it is the thighs of the African woman that serve as guide. And the narrator has no doubts about the pleasure of the experience. Wasn't it good? "*Yes. Yes.*" Within the same story, the narrator expresses his preference for a "full-bodied" woman, certainly a change from early works in which

Wideman's ideal woman was always slim (and most always European): "I want her robust, those wide hips and broad shoulders bumpered with flesh" (25). Seemingly, Wideman is turning his earlier notions of African women—ones based on a Eurocentric perspective—upside down, topsy-turvy. In fact, in "welcome," his image of them is switched in midstream, right in the middle of a sentence: "There was this fat girl in the Woodside. No, not fat. A big girl, solid, pretty, light on her feet, a large pretty big-eyed brown girl thirteen or fourteen with black crinkly hair and smooth kind of round chubby cheek babydoll face" (141–42). An earlier notion of the African woman, an earlier way of seeing, a "throwback" is revised in mid context to reflect the new consciousness Wideman has of himself and his people.

The intellectual who is Wideman in these stories is even more self-critical than the intellectuals in *Damballah* and *Philadelphia Fire*. He is also more conscious of the role he plays as a university professor and writer. In "Backseat," Wideman examines the significance of his using three names on his novels: "When I published my first novel, I wanted my father's name to be part of the record so I was John Edgar Wideman on the cover. Now the three names of my entities sound pretentious to me, stiff and old-fashioned. I'd prefer to be just plain John Wideman" (42). The words "just plain" are significant for they reflect Wideman's desire to be part of the masses, not distinct from them as in *Hurry Home*. In that novel as well as in the first, there is the suggestion that the three names were used not only because he wanted his father's name to be part of the record, but also because using them was a way of distinguishing himself as important, unique, a somebody distinct from and superior to other Africans. Now as an African-centered person, he sees no significant difference between himself and his people. Just how far Wideman has come from that early petty bourgeois intellectual position is demonstrated by his almost exclusive use of lower case letters for titles, and at times within the text itself, of the new stories in this collection. Moreover, the title of the book itself, *the stories of john edgar wideman,* is in lower case letters to reflect the humbling process, the Africological process, Wideman has experienced.

"signs" is a powerful story in its revelation of just how far Wideman has come in reclaiming his African Personality. It is a story about an African woman who is a professor at a predominantly

European university. Two incidents are revealed in the story or rather there is a story within a story. Both involve racism or its consequences. The incident that occurs first in time is one when the professor, Kendra Crawley, is harassed at graduate school, the only African in a girl's dorm: "When she's seen the first sign, a piece of cardboard thumbtacked to a door, she'd thought it was a joke, poor, poor taste, but a joke nonetheless, the *Whites Only* sign stuck to the communal bathroom door" (80). But she soon discovers it was no joke. The harassment continues and increases. Those who could come to her aid—African male graduate students—are "too tame, too bourgie, too white . . . No. They roomed in town where they could cop to their heart's content, tame, bourgie, white pussy in private" (82). Perhaps this indictment against young African men includes Wideman himself when he was a student at the University of Pennsylvania.

The second incident, the one that occurs when Kendra is a professor at a similar university, revolves around a discussion she has with one of her students, a European male who does not understand the relevance of studying Milton's *Paradise Lost*. Her reaction: she feels she's going to explode, dealing with "little blond, blue-eyed devil" European students (79). Why ask her the reason for making Milton a requirement. She too is following orders. If she had her "druthers," she would require that they read about the

> Rebel angels . . . Martin, Malcolm, Mandela. Saint Douglass. Saint Harriet. No, not Ozzie's wife, cracker. Ms. Tubman to you. If the syllabus of Western Civ ever tilted my way. Which it don't, boy. So ask your mama to apologize. Not me. She married the boss. Raised you. I was just someone to fetch his slippers. Iron his pants. A little action on the side. (78)

This Wideman is clearly not the same one who escaped to Laramie, Wyoming. Rather, the passage reveals a Wideman who would run from Laramie, skip over it entirely, if he could. Purge it from his memory.

Wideman's increased consciousness of the writing process—the use of form to enhance content, but perhaps most importantly, the use of form to reveal the consciousness of the author—is demonstrated throughout this collection. There are three significant examples: First, as mentioned, Wideman uses lower case letters for titles, an effort to minimize distinctions based on superiority or inferiority, between words as well as people. His name and most of the titles, including the title of the book, are in lower case letters. Secondly, Wideman arranges his stories so that the very arrangement conveys a message to the reader. By placing "a voice foretold" directly after "what he saw," Wideman implies that there is little difference between the nature of the African's oppression in South Africa and that in the U.S. For one thing, there is police brutality of the African community occurring in both countries. Third, he indicates that the mere writing process, although limited and long range in its impact, contributes to the liberation of African people: "Try as they might, they could not usurp her story. In her own good time, in words or deeds or fiery silence, the truth of her witness would be heard" ("Backseat," 30). Not only is truth liberating in itself, but also it will eventually come out, "be heard."

All in all, Wideman's process of reclaiming his African Personality continues in *the stories of john edgar wideman*. And if so, how can the works in this collection be less powerful, less liberated in form than those in *Damballah* as the *New York Times* critic contends? In 1992 Wideman knows more, has experienced more about the African's reality. Not only does he have a Homewood perspective, a "down home," "back home," perspective, but also an international one in regard to African people, a perspective which gives him the assurance to burst the traditional forms of fiction, to write an uninhibited, e.g., unpunctuated, text. So he is at ease in writing about the death of an African male struggling to survive in the streets of Homewood in "everybody knew bubba riff" or of writing in the voice of a newborn girl in "newborn thrown in trash and dies." How can these kinds of stories be considered conventional tales? So while there may be an absence of a "Faulknersque" quality to these stories, there is the presence of an "African-esque" one.

Notes

CHAPTER 1. JOHN EDGAR WIDEMAN: RECLAIMING THE AFRICAN PERSONALITY

1. The term *African* is used to refer to all people of African descent no matter where they happen to be born or happen to live in the world. The term *European* is used to refer to all people of European descent no matter where they happen to be born or happen to live in the world.

2. Molefi Kete Asante, *Afrocentricity: The Theory of Social Change* (Trenton, N.J.: Africa World Press, 1988), 4.

3. John Edgar Wideman, *Brothers and Keepers* (New York: Penguin, 1984). All page references are in the text.

4. The phrase "African Holocaust" was used by Maulana Karenga at the June 1991 Africological Conference at the University of Wisconsin–Milwaukee as a term that more appropriately describes the past experiences and present consequences of African people during the slave trade and slavery. The term "mfekane" is used also to refer to the slave trade, slavery, and colonialism as well as to their consequences, consequences still being felt today.

5. The definition of capitalism used here is one defined as an economic system characterized by "the concentration in a few hands of the ownership of the means of producing wealth and by unequal distribution of the products of human labour" (Walter Rodney, *How Europe Underdeveloped Africa*, 13). Emile Burns, in *An Introduction to Marxism*, defines it as a system "which divides society into classes [sections of people who get their living in the same way], one which carries out the production (slave, serf, wage-worker), while the other (slave-owner, lord, capitalist employer) enjoys a part of the product without having to work to produce it" (54). Both definitions are applicable here.

6. W. E. B. Du Bois, *The Souls of Black Folks*, in *Three Negro Classics* (New York: Avon Books, 1965), 214–15.

7. Marcus Garvey, quoted in Richard Barksdale and Keneth Kinnamon, *Black Writers of America* (New York: Macmillan, 1972), 570.

8. Amy Jacques Garvey, "Black is Beautiful," in *Voices of a Black Nation: Political Journalism in the Harlem Renaissance*, edited by Theodore Vincent (San Francisco: Ramparts, 1973), 373–74.

9. Western countries with "third world" colonies developed a policy of using colonial subjects to fight in world wars. Africans, for their part, saw these wars as their opportunity to "prove" their patriotism and, in return, expected to be treated better once they returned to their respective colonies. Chinweizu in *The West and the Rest of Us* examines one case in point:

Blaise Diagne of Senegal would even go as far as to exert himself in the defense of France, in the hope of alleviating the weight of French rule on Africans. When in 1917, as deputy from Senegal to the French National Assembly, he was asked by Georges Clemenceau to recruit troops from French Africa to help France fight off the Germans, who were then poised upon the Marne, Diagne accepted the task. He furnished France with close to a million black laborers and soldiers. Why? Diagne believed that if Africans came to the rescue and helped to save her, France might prove more liberal toward them. (85)

10. Frantz Fanon, *The Wretched of the Earth* (New York: Grove Press, 1967), 36–37.

11. Ibid., 46.

12. Ibid., 39 and 52.

13. Ibid., 45.

14. *Malcolm X, Malcolm X Speaks* (New York: Grove Press, 1965), 170.

15. Ibid., 168–69.

16. Kwame Nkrumah, *Consciencism: Philosophy and Ideology for Decolonization* (New York: Monthly Review Press, 1970), 79.

17. Ibid.

18. Ibid, 3–4.

19. Kay Bonetti, "An Interview with John Edgar Wideman," *The Missouri Review* 9.2 (1986): 85.

20. Carter G. Woodson, *The Mis-Education of the Negro* (Nashville, Tenn.: Winston-Derek Publishers, 1990), 56.

21. Bonetti, "Interview," 82.

22. Wilfred Samuels, "Going Home: A Conversation with John Edgar Wideman," *Callaloo* 6.1 (1983): 45.

23. Samuels, "Going Home," 43.

24. Wideman, "*Stomping the Blues:* Ritual in Black Music and Speech," *The American Poetry Review* 7: 45.

25. James W. Coleman, *Blackness and Modernism: The Literary Career of John Edgar Wideman* (Jackson: University Press of Mississippi, 1989), Appendix, 158–59.

26. John O'Brien, "John Wideman," in *Interviews with Black Writers* (New York: Liveright, 1973), 219.

27. Bonetti, "Interview," 80.

28. Coleman, *Blackness and Modernism*, 6.

29. Wideman, "Defining the Black Voice in Fiction," *Black American Literature Forum* 11: 81.

30. Coleman, *Blackness and Modernism*, Appendix, 152.

31. Ibid., 150.

32. Ibid., 160.

CHAPTER 2. "MEAN MEAN MEAN TO BE FREE": THE EVOLUTION OF WIDEMAN'S CONSCIOUSNESS

1. Fanon, *Wretched of the Earth*, 39.

2. O'Brien, "John Wideman," 213.

3. Bonetti, "Interview," 89.

4. Wideman, *A Glance Away* (New York: Holt, Rinehart and Winston, 1967). All page references are in the text.

5. Wideman, *Hurry Home* (New York: Henry Holt and Company, 1970). All page references are in the text.

6. O'Brien, "John Wideman," 218.

7. Coleman, *Blackness and Modernism,* 46.

8. Ibid., Appendix, 152.

9. Wideman, *The Lynchers* (New York: Henry Holt and Company, 1973). All page references are in the text.

10. In *The Lynchers* Wideman is still more interested in the idea of something more than its execution: theory over practice. It's more significant than that the planners have an idea for solving the African's dilemma. See O'Brien's interview of Wideman in which the novelist states: "In *The Lynchers* it doesn't make any difference whether the conspirators pull their plot off or not, it doesn't make any difference whether we have an Armageddon in America or not; what does matter is what certain social realities have pushed these characters to, what attitudes are taken by both blacks and whites. In fact, a subterranean apocalypse does come to pass because people are changed more by their imagination than they are by actual external events" (218). As in *Hurry Home,* Wideman believes that the imagination reigns supreme over reality. Perhaps it's this kind of early thinking that allows him to justify his marriage to Judy; his move to Laramie, Wyoming; and his estrangement from his people.

11. James W. Coleman has a different interpretation of Littleman's physical appearance: "Wideman uses Littleman's crippled body to make a statement about the conspirators' unrealistic attempts to change the external world of the black community. Littleman can present an illusion of himself while he is sitting at the bar, and his smooth talk is enough to excite a prostitute about the possibilities. But the withered legs cannot maneuver him into position to demonstrate what he believes is his sexual prowess" (*Blackness and Modernism,* 50).

12. Coleman, *Blackness and Modernism,* 64.

13. In a 1983 interview with Wilfred Samuels, Wideman speaks of the "vivid clarity" he possessed when writing *Hiding Place:* "Specifically, something happened with *Hiding Place* that had never happened before. I saw the ending of the novel just as clear in my mind as I see images on television or in the movies. It came to me with just such direct, vivid clarity. . . . In a space of about ten minutes, the whole story was in my mind" (47). Unencumbered by the extra baggage of Eurocentricity, Wideman is like a person who has removed his blinders.

14. Bonetti, "Interview," 95.

15. Robby's involvement in armed robbery occurred on 15 November 1975; *Damballah* and *Hiding Place* were published in 1981, eight years after *The Lynchers.* The reader cannot help but to make a connection between this hiatus and the straightforward (because Wideman was shocked into an awareness of his African identity?) writing in *Hiding Place.*

16. Wideman, *Hiding Place* (New York: Vintage, 1981). All page references are in the text.

17. Coleman seems to think that Bess is transformed more significantly by her repetition of events, words, and phrases than by Tommy's comments and urgings: "Bess is transformed to a significant extent because she repeats over and over to herself, and to Tommy, important events of the past, family connections, and key words and phrases that link her and Tommy to the past and magically make him materialize for her as a relative; she does not accept him as a relative during the first section of the book" (*Blackness and Modernism*, 65–66). Coleman here seems to rely on magic, similar to the magic used in Wideman's novels, in interpreting the text. The text suggests that Bess realizes right away that Tommy is a relative. And it is he who pushes her to remember, to make the connections necessary in her healing process.

18. See John O'Brien for a different interpretation of the ending of *Hiding Place*: "As one has come to expect in Wideman's fiction, the ending of *Hiding Place* is left somewhat unclear. My reading of the novel suggests that Bess accidentally sets herself on fire, that her shack burns down, and that Tommy is shot by police as soon as he leaves Bess. Yet, as Bess is dying, she imagines herself going to Tommy's rescue (i.e., 'coming out of hiding'), to insist upon his innocence" ("The Presence of the Past," *Callaloo* 6.1 [1983]: 170).

19. Wideman, *Damballah* (New York: Vintage, 1981). All page references are in the text.

20. Coleman, *Blackness and Modernism*, 95.

21. Wideman, *Sent for You Yesterday* (New York: Vintage, 1983). All page references are in the text.

22. Because Brother is rooted in the African community, he also serves as a mirror for it. Not so much reflecting physical features, Brother reveals the characters' past and present, strengths and weaknesses. In an interview with Kay Bonetti, Wideman states: "In a funny way he's a mirror, but you can't see through him. He's not a glass. He's solid. But he has the qualities of a spirit, he's immaterial. He doesn't have blood but everybody's afraid that when they look in there they'll see through his skin. And of course if they see through his skin what they'll see is their own mortality, their creaturehood, their own blood" (95–96).

23. Wideman, *Reuben* (New York: Penguin, 1987). All page references are in the text.

24. Coleman points out that "Reuben gives himself only a first name and structures a mythic existence that will produce the values and attitudes he needs to spur him to action in black people's lives" (*Blackness and Modernism*, 131). But the most significant point, it seems, lies in the fact that Wideman creates a character with only one name and that name means savior. Reuben is the savior of his race; at least, he attempts to be. In Coleman's interview of Wideman, the latter states that Reuben "is an intermediary. He is in the battleground. It's his job to untangle people from the negative effects of the dominant culture, to protect people from one another and also from these invidious forces that are all around them" (Appendix, 151).

25. The "brother" image is strong in *Reuben*. Just as Reuben's brother is incarcerated, so is Wideman's. Both Reuben and Wideman seem to use the image of their jailed brothers as a spark to perform some significant act for the African

community. In the Bonetti interview, Wideman admits that "the idea of connecting oneself to a literal brother or to other people on earth is probably about the
only notion that's going to have any chance of saving us all" (103).

26. On 12 May 1985, Philadelphia Mayor Wilson Goode delivered the com-
mencement address at Hampton University in Hampton, Virginia. The essence
of his speech was "don't forget where you come from." Africans graduating
from college must be socially responsible to the African community. On 13 May
1985, Mayor Goode approved the bombing of the MOVE house on Osage Avenue in Philadelphia. The bomb killed eleven of the thirteen members (including
women and children) who were in the house and shattered homes within blocks.

The MOVE organization got its start at the end of the Civil Rights Movement
and the beginning of the Black Power Movement. In the late 1960s and early
1970s, an African named Vincent Leaphart was known as a philosopher and
lover of animals. One of his first disciples was a European named Donald J.
Glassey. Together they founded an organization that would come to be known
as MOVE (not an acronym). MOVE called itself a religious revolutionary organization and all members used the surname "Africa" (*The Nkrumaist*, 1, 7).

27. Wideman, *Philadelphia Fire* (New York: Henry Holt and Company, 1990).
All page references are in the text.

CHAPTER 3. "AND ARN'T I A WOMAN": WIDEMAN'S WOMEN

1. Sojourner Truth, "And Arn't I a Woman," in *Cavalcade*, ed. Arthur P.
Davis and Saunders Redding (Boston: Houghton Mifflin Company, 1971).

2. Perhaps digression is not an accurate term in this case, since Wideman
admits on several occasions that all three works in the Homewood Trilogy were
conceived simultaneously. It may be more appropriate to state that thus far the
contradictions in Wideman's canon in regard to women continue to be present.

3. In fact, Wideman seems unable to reconcile physical beauty with strength
of character. It also seems difficult for him to see the beauty in women with
African characteristics.

4. Wideman is exposed to another set of beauty standards during his visits
with Robby. And just as the author re-evaluates other accepted beliefs and values
with the help of Robby, it is not far-fetched to think that Robby's emphasis on
the beauty of African women impacted upon Wideman as well. In fact, Wideman
includes Robby's poem "Hey, Sister" in *Brothers and Keepers:*

> I see you there behind your mask
>   Of powder and your store-bought hair
> I see a light that shines as a star
>   That comes from over there
> That place we were before we
>   Came over here
> I feel the warmth that still comes from you
>   Though your emotions are freezing in white snow

Sister you can be a leader too
        Wipe away your false colors
Wear your blackness Queen.

                                                    (205)

5. In *Women, Race & Class*, Angela Davis discusses the rise of the ideology of femininity in regard to European women:

As the ideology of femininity—a by-product of industrialization—was popularized and disseminated through the new ladies' magazines and romantic novels, white women came to be seen as inhabitants of a sphere totally severed from the realm of productive work. The cleavage between the home and the public economy, brought on by industrial capitalism, established female inferiority more firmly than ever before. "Woman" became synonymous in the prevailing propaganda with "mother" and "housewife," and both "mother" and "housewife" bore the fatal mark of inferiority. But among Black female slaves, this vocabulary was nowhere to be found. The economic arrangements of slavery contradicted the hierarchical sexual roles incorporated in the new ideology. (12)

CHAPTER 4. "THE MIS-EDUCATION OF THE NEGRO": THE INTELLECTUAL AND THE COMMUNITY

1. Woodson, *Mis-Education of the Negro*, 35.
2. Some scholars have referred to that "I'm the only one" mentality of African intellectuals as a petty bourgeois mentality resulting from capitalism. In "The Role of the Intelligentsia," Toks Adewale explains this type of thinking:

As a result of the philosophy stemming from bourgeois individualism, which is ancillary to the capitalist mode of production, many African students and especially members of the African intelligentsia in general believe that they have achieved their elevated status above the masses of African people merely through their own individual initiative. This way of thinking is backward and leads to false conclusions. For if the African intelligentsia has primarily itself to credit for its socio-economic "success," logic would suggest that it has only itself to serve since it was simply through its own efforts that it has entered a life of comfort and leisure. No lie is as far from the truth as this one is. The truth of the matter is that at no time in the history of African people have we lacked individual initiative to be realized. And it is without a doubt that the opportunities, albeit small, that the intelligentsia in particular and other members of the African bourgeoisie in general benefit from are a result of the courageous and relentless struggle of the masses of our people for human dignity and progress. (2)

3. Coleman, *Blackness and Modernism*, 44.
4. Ibid., 77.
5. Ibid., 79–80.
6. *Damballah* is also useful in showing the reader that the conscientizing process for Wideman is not complete at the time of its writing. For as Coleman states, John's advice to Tommy, when the latter runs to Wyoming to give himself up, "almost implies that Tommy will be treated by the law in the same way as a

white man. Such confusion of reality is almost as bad as anything that has happened to Tommy" (93).

7. Coleman, *Blackness and Modernism,* 119.

CHAPTER 5. THINKING BLACK, WRITING RAP: WIDEMAN AND THE WRITING PROCESS

1. Coleman, *Blackness and Modernism,* Appendix 148–49.
2. Bonetti, "Interview," 88.
3. Samuels, "Going Home," 44.
4. Bonetti, "Interview," 100.
5. Bonetti, "Interview," 86.
6. For Wideman's view of this theory of the musician who helps us make sense of reality, see Coleman, Appendix, 154–155.
7. Coleman, Appendix 156.
8. Ellison, *Shadow and Act* (New York: Random House, 1953), 223.
9. Henry Louis Gates, Jr., *The Signifying Monkey: A Theory of African-American Literary Criticism* (New York: Oxford University Press, 1988), 60 and 88.
10. Ibid., xxvi.
11. Ibid., 181.
12. Wideman, *"Stomping the Blues,"* 44 and 45.
13. Bonetti, "Interview," 102.

CHAPTER 6. "HOW WOULD *THEY* KNOW?": CONCLUSION

1. Review of *the stories of john edgar wideman* in the *New York Times,* 21 July 1992, B2.
2. Frantz Fanon, *Black Skin, White Masks* (New York: Grove Press, 1967), 38.
3. Wideman, *the stories of john edgar wideman* (New York: Pantheon, 1992). All page references are in the text.
4. It is interesting that Wideman chooses an infant girl rather than boy as his protagonist, for not only are African youth most oppressed in our society, but also, within this sector of the population, the African female youth are most vulnerable. This choice reflects Wideman's increased consciousness of the plight of the African female. Clearly, Wideman is thinking of the problems confronting African people and possible solutions for them at this stage in his writing career.
5. Significantly, there are no European female characters in these new stories. Contrasted with his earlier works, from *A Glance Away* to *Sent for You Yesterday,* this omission is quite a useful gauge of Wideman's "new thinking."

Bibliography

Adewale, Toks. "The Role of the Intelligentsia." Unpublished Paper. September 1982.

Asante, Molefi Kete. *Afrocentricity: The Theory of Social Change.* Trenton, N.J: Africa World Press, 1988.

Barksdale, Richard and Keneth Kinnamon. *Black Writers of America.* New York: Macmillan, 1972.

Bennion, John. "The Shape of Memory in John Edgar Wideman's *Sent for You Yesterday.*" *Black American Literature Forum* 20. 1/2 (1986): 143–50.

Bonetti, Kay. "An Interview with John Edgar Wideman." *The Missouri Review* 9. 2 (1986): 75–103.

Burns, Emile. *An Introduction to Marxism.* New York: International Publishers, 1969.

Chinweizu. *The West and the Rest of Us.* New York: Vintage, 1975.

Coleman, James W. *Blackness and Modernism: The Literary Career of John Edgar Wideman.* Jackson: University Press of Mississippi, 1989.

Davis, Angela Y. *Women, Race & Class.* New York: Vintage, 1983.

Du Bois, W. E. B. "The Souls of Black Folks." In *Three Negro Classics.* New York: Avon Books, 1965.

Ellison, Ralph. *Shadow and Act.* New York: Random House, 1953.

Fanon, Frantz. *Black Skin, White Masks.* New York: Grove Press, Inc., 1967.

Fanon, Frantz. *The Wretched of the Earth.* New York: Grove Press, Inc., 1963.

Garvey, Amy Jacques. "Black Is Beautiful." In *Voices of a Black Nation: Political Journalism in the Harlem Renaissance.* Edited by Theodore Vincent. San Francisco: Ramparts, 1973.

Garvey, Marcus. *Philosophy and Opinions of Marcus Garvey.* London: Frank Cass and Company Limited, 1983.

Gates, Henry Louis, Jr. *The Signifying Monkey: A Theory of African-American Literary Criticism.* New York: Oxford, 1988.

Malcolm X. *Malcolm X Speaks.* New York: Grove Press, Inc., 1965.

"Move: Now We Must Move On!!" *The Nkrumaist.* November-December 1985, pp. 1, 7.

Nkrumah, Kwame. *Consciencism: Philosophy and Ideology for Decolonization.* New York: Monthly Review Press, 1970.

O'Brien, John, ed. "John Wideman." In *Interviews with Black Writers.* New York: Liveright, 1973.

O'Brien, John. "The Presence of the Past." *Callaloo* 6. 1 (1983): 168–71.

Rodney, Walter. *How Europe Underdeveloped Africa.* Dar es Salaam, Tanzania: Tanzania Publishing House, 1972.

Samuels, Wilfred. "Going Home: A Conversation with John Edgar Wideman." *Callaloo* 6. 1 (1983): 40–59.

Tate, Claudia. "Toni Morrison." In *Black Women Writers at Work.* New York: Continuum, 1985.

Truth, Sojourner. "And Arn't I A Woman." In *Calvacade,* edited by Arthur P. Davis and Saunders Redding. Boston: Houghton Mifflin Company, 1971.

Wideman, John Edgar. *A Glance Away.* New York: Holt, Rinehart and Winston, 1967.

———. *Brothers and Keepers.* New York: Penguin, 1984.

———. *Damballah.* New York: Vintage, 1981.

———. "Defining the Black Voice in Fiction." *Black American Literature Forum* 11: 79–82.

———. *Fever.* New York: Penguin, 1989.

———. *Hiding Place.* New York: Vintage, 1981.

———. *Hurry Home.* New York: Henry Holt and Company, 1970.

———. *The Lynchers.* New York: Henry Holt and Company, 1973.

———. *Philadelphia Fire.* New York: Henry Holt and Company, 1990.

———. *Reuben.* New York: Penguin, 1987.

———. *Sent for You Yesterday.* New York: Vintage, 1983.

———. "*Stomping the Blues*: Ritual in Black Music and Speech." *The American Poetry Review* 7: 42–45.

———. *the stories of john edgar wideman.* New York: Pantheon, 1992.

Woodson, Carter G. *The Mis-Education of the Negro.* Nashville, Tennessee: Winston-Derek Publishers, Inc., 1990.

Index

131